CULTURAL POLICY

David Bell and Kate Oakley survey the major debates emerging in cultural policy research, adopting an approach based on spatial scale to explore cultural policy at city, national and international level. They contextualise these discussions with an exploration of what both 'culture' and 'policy' mean when they are joined together as cultural policy.

Drawing on topical examples and contemporary research, as well as their own experience in both academia and consultancy, Bell and Oakley urge readers to think critically about the project of cultural policy as it is currently being played out around the world.

Cultural Policy is a comprehensive and readable book that provides a lively, up-to-date overview of key debates in cultural policy, making it ideal for students of media and cultural studies, creative and cultural industries, and arts management.

David Bell is Senior Lecturer in Critical Human Geography at the University of Leeds.

Kate Oakley is Professor of Cultural Policy at the University of Leeds.

KEY IDEAS IN MEDIA AND CULTURAL STUDIES

The *Key Ideas in Media and Cultural Studies* series covers the main concepts, issues, debates and controversies in contemporary media and cultural studies. Titles in the series constitute authoritative, original essays rather than literary surveys, but are also written explicitly to support undergraduate teaching. The series provides students and teachers with lively and original treatments of key topics in the field.

Cultural Policy by David Bell and Kate Oakley

Forthcoming:

Reality Television by Annette Hill
Culture by Ben Highmore
Celebrity by Sean Redmond
Representation by Jenny Kidd
Mediatization by Andreas Hepp

CULTURAL POLICY

David Bell and Kate Oakley

Routledge
Taylor & Francis Group

LONDON AND NEW YORK

First published 2015
by Routledge
2 Park Square, Milton Park, Abingdon, Oxon OX14 4RN

and by Routledge
711 Third Avenue, New York, NY 10017

Routledge is an imprint of the Taylor & Francis Group, an informa business

© 2015 David Bell and Kate Oakley

British Library Cataloguing in Publication Data
A catalogue record for this book is available from the British Library

Library of Congress Cataloging in Publication Data
Bell, David, 1965 February 12-
Cultural policy / David Bell and Kate Oakley.
pages cm -- (Key ideas in media and cultural studies)
1. Cultural policy. 2. Cultural policy--Research. I. Oakley, Kate. II. Title.
CB430.B436 2014
306--dc23
2014003127

ISBN: 978-0-415-66500-1 (hbk)
ISBN: 978-0-415-66501-8 (pbk)
ISBN: 978-0-203-12997-5 (ebk)

Typeset in Garamond
by Taylor and Francis Books

CONTENTS

TABLES

ACKNOWLEDGEMENTS

David: Thanks to all the students and teachers with whom I have discussed cultural policy over the years, especially those on the module Cultural Policy and Institutions at Staffordshire University, which is where this whole thing began for me. Also at Staffs, thanks to CTU colleagues for adventures in consultancy. To family and friends, especially Daisy, for keeping the cultural studies flame alight, and Corin, for introducing me to whole new worlds of culture. Thanks also to Natalie Foster, Sheni Kruger and all at Routledge who helped get this book made. And finally, to Kate – the perfect co-author.

Kate: First, thanks to David, whose project this was initially and who has been an excellent companion throughout. Second, thanks to all colleagues at the Institute of Communications Studies in Leeds for making it such a conducive place to work. To cultural policy mates Graham Hitchen and Tom Campbell for breakfast and good chats. And finally, thanks to Pete for everything else.

1

INTRODUCING CULTURAL POLICY

> Getting to know cultural policy and intervening in it is an important part of participating in culture.
>
> (Miller and Yudice 2002: 34)

In the final stages of writing this book, two new publications landed in our inboxes. Both have a lot to tell us, in different ways, about the project of cultural policy as it currently stands. Both also have things to tell us about the stuff of cultural policy; indeed, they are the stuff of cultural policy – they are both members of that sometimes loose category, 'policy documents' – and they are equally the stuff of cultural policy research: they are underpinned by the work of researchers (some named, others anonymous), they deploy empirical research in order to build a case for culture, and they quickly become the source text for further research, critique and discussion (this chapter included). The two publications are UNESCO's *Creative Economy Report*, billed as a 2013 Special Edition and subtitled *Widening Local Development Pathways*, and another 'special', this time from the European Commission: Special Eurobarometer 399, *Cultural Access and Participation*.

As a way into this book, we want to look at these two reports here. We'll begin with the Eurobarometer report, and here we want to use the publication to think about engagement with cultural policy and with culture, echoing Miller and Yudice's (2002) claim that opens this chapter. The *Cultural Access and Participation* Report is a collation of research findings, based on questionnaire surveys and interviews, detailing the extent of engagement in cultural activities among citizens from the 27 EU member states. To do this, it calculates very high, high, medium and low overall rates of cultural engagement, and then provides details of the types of cultural activity. The list of chosen activities is itself revealing – see Table 1.1.

As Chapter 2 details, the list drawn up by Eurobarometer is indicative of a number of tensions in the field of cultural policy – the tension between 'high' and 'popular' culture is the most obvious. But this first list only considers cultural consumption; the report later adds in research into cultural production (it uses the narrower term 'involvement in artistic activities'). Here again is a telling list for respondents to choose from (see Table 1.2).

It's interesting – to us at least – that the first list specifies watching or listening to a *cultural* programme on the TV or radio, and that the second list specifies doing *creative* computing such as web design or blogging. As we'll see later, the contentious issue of defining the remit of cultural policy comes down, at least in part, to defining culture.

Table 1.1 Categories of cultural consumption in the Eurobarometer report: respondents were asked to state how many times in the last 12 months they had undertaken each activity.

Watched or listened to a cultural programme on the TV or radio	Been to a concert
Read a book	Visited a public library
Been to the cinema	Been to the theatre
Visited a historical monument or site	Seen a ballet, dance performance or an opera
Visited a museum or gallery	

Source: Eurobarometer 2013

Table 1.2 Categories of artistic activities in the Eurobarometer report: respondents were asked to indicate which of these they had done, alone or as part of a group or class, in the last 12 months.

Danced	Done creative computing such as designing websites or blogs, etc.
Made a film, done some photography, sung	Written a poem, an essay, a novel, etc.
Done any other artistic activities such as sculpture, painting, handicrafts or drawing	Acted on the stage or in a film Other
Played a musical instrument	None

Source: Eurobarometer 2013

We'll also discuss the parallel problem of defining policy. To what extent is the Eurobarometer Report really a policy document? Well, we would argue that it represents an important strand within cultural policy research: the measuring of culture. The introduction to the report explicitly grounds its mission in the context of existing EU directives on culture, quoting from the Treaty on the European Union and the EU's Agenda for Culture. It is a follow-up to a 2007 survey and so aims to look at changing participation over time, with a view to assessing the success (or otherwise) of the EU's Agenda and its related Culture Programme. So, it belongs to the growing body of cultural audits, which have bloomed in the so-called era of New Public Management (Belfiore 2004). Its slightly grander stated aim is to explore and measure 'how EU citizens think and behave in the area of culture' (Eurobarometer 2013: 2), though it is quite a leap from simple statistics on dancing or reading to *thinking*.

We should add two further, typically EU dimensions of the report: first, it wants to look for proxy measures of European integration via cultural participation, so it also surveys the extent to which culture crosses borders in Europe, and here it looks at the movement of people (going to a theatre in another EU country, for example) and the movement of cultural products (asking whether respondents have read a novel written in another EU country, for instance). In line with other cross-border initiatives in the EU (see Chapter 5), the report sees cultural exchange as evidence of increasing Europeanisation and a positive outcome of policies aiming for greater cooperation between nations. Second, the report singles out for analysis the role of the Internet for 'cultural purposes' – again, this is tricky definitional work, so it breaks these purposes down into 'direct' and 'indirect' use: the former would include reading an article online, the latter online shopping for cultural goods.

The publication of the report in November 2013 did not go unnoticed – though the uptake of 'cultural' news stories by the media is a very uneven, sometimes unpredictable business. Its coverage on British national TV news caught our attention. Here, the main findings that became newsworthy were the statistics on levels of cultural participation in the UK compared with some of our near neighbours (and sometime rivals). A TV newscaster summarised that new research had shown that Brits are 'more cultural' than both the French and the Italians. And this isn't wholly untrue: in six of the nine categories listed in Table 1.1, reported participation rates for the UK are higher than those in either France or Italy. But the framing of this story played on longer-standing prejudices and stereotypes (the French castigating the British for being uncultured 'Rosbifs'; Italy as self-proclaimed cultural capital of Europe, etc.). For viewers who grew up watching *Jeux Sans Frontières* and *Eurovision*, like us, the familiarly jokey tone was instantly recognisable. The proof is in: Brits win again! We visit more art galleries than the Italians and are better read than the French! (The news skated over the fact that highest participation rates were found in Scandinavian countries.) Of course, this is a crass oversimplification of the detailed cultural statistics presented in the report, but it's also revealing of the ways cultural policy can hit the headlines.

One way in which cultural policy has been hitting the headlines during our time writing this book has been in the context of the economic crisis and resulting public sector cuts. And the Eurobarometer and UNESCO reports both acknowledge that times are hard in the cultural field, for both producers and consumers. While UNESCO foregrounds 'economy' in its report's title, the contents actually signify a shift of emphasis away from what has been the dominant discourse of the last twenty years or so – seeing culture as part of a standard economic growth model – to, as the subtitle of the report suggests, one that seeks to position cultural activities within a variety of economic development models.

As this book makes clear, the rationales which drive cultural policy vary according to time, place and political context. Recent decades have seen economic drivers – the growth of the cultural sectors and their ability to generate profits and jobs – come to the forefront in many countries, variously described as the cultural industries, creative industries or creative economy. These terms actually connote different emphases, but over time the focus on culture as a driver of economic growth has become the dominant one for both national governments and international organisations such as the EU and United Nations. From the late 1990s, the 'creative industries' idea in particular began to achieve international traction (Cunningham 2009), including in the Global South, which might be assumed to have been suspicious of an idea so clearly fashioned in the Global North.

Like much of the rest of our economies, however, culture-led economic growth has proved highly unequal in the distribution of benefits; recognising and responding to this is at the core of UNESCO's 2013 *Creative Economy Report*. It makes it clear that we cannot just assume that developing the cultural industries will lead to a more balanced, fairer economy. While artists based anywhere can develop products for global markets, finance and access to distribution networks and specialist legal and others skills are still concentrated in a few global centres. Within countries, cultural production is sometimes concentrated in a few large urban centres, and access to culture is geographically skewed towards wealthier areas and those with larger populations. At the same time, the recent policy focus on economic rationales may have obscured the other vital roles that culture plays in our lives and our societies – as education, identity, spirituality, or even fun.

The *Creative Economy Report* attempts to move away from this 'creative industries' model, towards a more pluralistic view of economic development. This acknowledges the growth of commercial popular culture across the world – Tanzanian hip hop, Mexican telenovelas, Nigerian moviemaking, South Korean pop music and so on – but also recognises that there are different kinds of economic models, from co-operatives and non-profits to individual lifestyle business, barter or sharing systems, and that these may offer more appropriate models for cultural activities which represent other sources of value for people beyond the economic. The way in which this shift will be recognised or taken up by national governments, city authorities or community and activist groups remains to be seen (see Chapter 3 for the question of who makes cultural policy). But if it is influential, it will represent yet another iteration in the developing project of cultural policy.

THE PROJECT OF CULTURAL POLICY

This books concerns itself with asking not just what is cultural policy and how does it operate, but also *what is it for?* We think it is important for students of this subject to understand the wider political and social context in which policy is made, and the responsibility of policymakers, academics, cultural workers, activists, managers and consumers to think about and engage with these questions. Cultural policy is a form of public policy, as this book makes clear, and it is subject to the same political changes, financial challenges and global tensions as any other form of public policy (and arguably more than some).

Let's take one example. The degree to which the global economic crisis which began in 2007/8 represents a fatal challenge to the prevailing model of capitalism is of course a matter of intense dispute (for different takes on this see, for example, Häring and Douglas 2012; Mirowski 2013; Turner 2012). But what is indisputable is that it has represented a profound shock to that model and will have lasting consequences for the form of welfare capitalism that has prevailed, particularly in Europe, in the decades following the Second World War. It is within that model of state spending on public goods such as health, education and public transport that the understanding of cultural policy that shapes this book has arisen. It assumes a role for the state in funding both cultural production and consumption; how those funding decisions are made, by whom and for what purposes is one of the subjects of our book. But in many Global North economies, particularly in Europe, states have almost bankrupted themselves paying for the costs of the financial crisis, and state spending on goods like culture is likely to be constrained for some time to come. Cuts to arts funding have been another way in which cultural policy has hit the headlines in recent times.

Adair Turner (2012) argues rightly that this move away from the state project of culture began before the financial crisis, when economic drivers of cultural policy came to the fore and the assumed beneficiary of policy switched from the nation, community or citizen to the entrepreneur, commercial organisation or individual consumer. He sees this as a change in the *politics* of cultural policy from what was essentially a communal focus to one which is more individualised, and from one which had at its heart the notion of a public good to one which is primarily concerned with promoting commercial success and market transactions. As the ability of states to maintain public spaces for culture and fund non-market provision becomes limited by financial constraints, it could be that we are moving to a world where cultural policy simply becomes economic regulation – treating culture in much the same way as policies that regulate the market for food or pharmaceuticals.

We think this is undesirable, and the UNESCO report suggests that some policymakers do too. This book argues that cultural policy remains at its heart an ethical and political project. We remain convinced of the vital importance of both critically interrogating and engaging with the world of cultural policy. Its role in shaping our lives is too important to brush off as 'over' – and there's a political danger there, that if we don't keep paying close attention to what is happening in cultural policy, we may end up with either a market-led system with minimal regulation or with decisions taken 'on our behalf' or 'in our interest' that are in reality neither of those things. We therefore hope that this book encourages the continued practices of getting to know and intervening in cultural policy, including by studying it.

APPROACHING CULTURAL POLICY

As you'll see throughout this book, the field of cultural policy studies is a large and rather complicated one. Despite some critics suggesting that its 'moment' has passed, perhaps eclipsed now by a creative economy approach of the type used by UNESCO (Turner 2014), we would like to counter-argue that the field is alive and well, and continuing to develop. Surveying recent publications, and looking at the breadth of university courses studying cultural policy, we see a heterogeneous body of knowledge that crosses disciplines and mixes methods. Attempting to summarise what he sees out there, Clive Gray (2010) provides a detailed sketch which we want to reproduce in full (minus the many citations to others' work he includes) because it indicates something of the heterogeneity (even promiscuity) of the interests of cultural policy researchers. Cultural policy, he writes, is concerned with:

> Community cultural development, cultural diversity, cultural sustain-ability, cultural heritage, the cultural and creative industries, lifestyle culture and eco-culture, planning for the intercultural city, cultural planning *per se*, support for national languages, 'currently controversial issues in the wider society', the 'culture wars' in the USA, 'the production of cultural citizens' as well as being concerned with 'representation, meaning and interpretation' and being a 'transhistorical political function'.
>
> (Gray 2010: 218)

Such a list of possible directions for cultural policy research to follow means that choices have to be made, structures imposed, boundaries drawn around the object of our study if we are ever going to partially summarise it – which is one aim of this book. Several possibilities present themselves: historical sweeps, sectoral discussions, a focus on particular cultural forms and practices … . But, perhaps because one of us is a geographer, we have adopted a novel approach to organising the material that constitutes the field of cultural policy: we have deployed the scaffold of spatial scale. Now, we need to acknowledge (and then largely sidestep) the ongoing debates in 'critical' human geography about scale: its definition, form, usefulness, whether it even exists (see Herod 2010 for a summary). For us, scale works as a handy device to organise and think through cultural policy. And to some extent we are not alone: several other scholars have alluded to the importance of thinking spatially or geographically about cultural policy. For example, Dave O'Brien (2013) highlights the geographical dimension to arts funding, and chooses one particular scale – the urban – for extended interrogation. Earlier, with co-author Steven Miles, he considered both local and regional scales in a discussion of cultural policy in England's 'peripheral north' (O'Brien and Miles 2010). Their interest here was in local implementation of policy, encouraging a place-specific analysis that in turn unpacks the role of cultural policy in definitions of space and place. In comparing Liverpool with NewcastleGateshead, O'Brien and Miles conclude that the 'local' and place-specific is an important but underexplored aspect of cultural policy, contesting any notion of a creeping homogenisation taking place as policy 'rolls out' across the country. And UNESCO (2013) gestures to scale at the end of its latest *Creative Economy Report*, in a discussion that tracks from the global to the national and then the local. Similarly, in the context of creative industries policy, Michael Volkering (2001: 437) draws our attention to the 'territorial nature of policy', and seeks to explore policy 'as a territorial or spatial concept' (440), for example through the metaphor of 'mapping' or through notions of 'boundaries'. But this is more than metaphorical: policy is shaped by and also shapes geography. We should add that this emphasis on territoriality does not mean we need only study policies in place; we need also to deploy a relational analysis, looking across and between scales. For, as McCann and Ward argue:

> Policymaking must be understood as both relational and territorial, as both in motion and simultaneously fixed, or embedded in place. The contradictory nature of policy should not, however, be seen as detrimental to its operation. Rather, the tension between policy as relational and dynamic, on the one hand, and fixed and territorial, on the other, is a productive one. It is a necessary tension that produces policy and places.
>
> (McCann and Ward 2011: xv)

Keen observers and scale-spotters will have already noticed our selective and partial use of scalar architecture in the chapters that follow: we have chosen to explore cultural policy through only three scales – the urban, the national and the international. Depending on the version of spatial scale you prefer (we have chosen one used in a previous life to discuss geographies of food; see Bell and Valentine 1997), we have missed out various scales. Here we'd like to partly remedy that by thinking through the scales we don't think through later. So, our chosen scalar architecture in full runs like this: body-home-community-city-region-nation-global. Let's start with home. We've already mentioned home in this introduction, in fact: in terms of watching television (whether the viewing habits of Eurobaromoter respondents or our own TV news watching). Cultural policy enters the home in many and various ways. It enters it on the airwaves and in acts of cultural consumption that bring books, comics, CDs, blogs and all manner of cultural goods and experiences into domestic space. One way or another, our homes are full of cultural policy, though this is rarely self-evident.

But sometimes it is more obvious. One day in October 2013, David was standing outside the City Art Gallery in his hometown of Leeds when he saw an unusual sight: passers-by, heading to and from the art gallery, clutching strange oversized bags. What was in the bags? Paintings. These folk were members of the gallery's picture lending scheme, which for fifty years has allowed local citizens to borrow art works from the scheme's collection to hang at home for three months, before returning them and choosing again.[1] This curious sight on an autumnal Saturday lunchtime gives us a rather particular example of cultural policy entering domestic space, therefore, but it carries with it many of the threads that tie together cultural policy – ideas about access, about the uses and value of culture – and literally brings them home. And as numerous cultural surveys have revealed, much of our cultural activity does take place at home (see Chapter 2 on the Taking Part survey in the UK). But lending people art to display at home reiterates some more problematic notions of high versus popular culture, too (see also Painter 2002): while *Taking Part* records that over 90 per cent of Britons say that watching TV is their main leisure activity, watching TV and looking at art do not have the same 'cultural value' – hence Eurobarometer's narrow definition of watching 'cultural' programmes as an indicator of cultural participation (of course, this only prompts more definitional anxiety: is something like *Strictly*

Come Dancing 'cultural', given that dance is a core category in the Eurobarometer data?) So, while we have not included home as a scalar category in this book, we must acknowledge here that for many people the domestic setting is where they encounter the out-workings of cultural policy, whether in terms of broadcasting regulation and copyright law, or ploughing through the endless cultural materials online, or the borrowing of paintings.

The scale of the body is one that has often been neglected in geographical analyses, and arguably has received less attention as a site of cultural policy, too. Yet some scholars have shown how certain bodily attributes – deportment, manners, affects and emotions – have undoubtedly been the target of cultural policy, whether in terms of stirring national pride or in disciplining certain people into more 'civilised' forms of behaviour. In particular, Tony Bennett's Foucauldian work on cultural institutions has revealed their role in shaping subjects (Bennett 1995, 1998). While this work is often about institutional spaces, such as museums, it also draws our attention to the bodily scale, to cultural policy as embodied in behaviours and actions reshaped through encounter with culture. We all come to learn, for example, how to 'behave' in an art gallery – how to stand, how long to stare at a painting, the right gestures and expressions, the noises we can and can't make: we learn to do 'gallerying' as a particular mode of bodily activity. (Perhaps taking art home is a way of avoiding such discipline?) Since it would be uncontentious to say that culture is expressed through the body, then perhaps it is unsurprising that cultural policy should also have a role to play in making and remaking bodies.

When it comes to the scales of community and the region, we would argue that we have included these throughout our discussion rather than in separate chapters. In the case of community, this surfaces a number of times in the chapters that follow, as an ebbing and flowing concern of cultural policy – though the history of 'community' as a concept within cultural policy demands fuller attention. Sometimes used as a synonym for 'the people' (as in, for example, 'community arts'), sometimes to tag a specific cultural sector (such as the 'arts community') and sometimes as a formal aggregation bound by treaties (as in the European Community),

community has been variously mobilised and articulated to culture and cultural policy, though with little consistency. In the case of the region, we do discuss this explicitly several times, in so doing revealing a problem with the region as a spatial concept: where does it fit? Clearly, as our discussion in chapters 5 and 6 shows, there are different ways of thinking about and locating the region; in some cases, it is viewed as a subnational scale – as in O'Brien and Miles' (2010) discussion of England's 'peripheral north', or Allen *et al.*'s (1998) work on the southeast. The partial devolution of arts administration to the English regions is perhaps the best-known example of explicit subnational regional cultural policy in recent UK history (Gray 2000). At other times, the region is definitionally supranational, as in the case of the EU which we explore through both national and international lenses. The Eurobarometer Report we looked at earlier both holds together a single EU region and begins to pull it apart, repeatedly drawing distinctions between northern and southern Europe (and between nations). And the emphasis in the UNESCO report on South-South cooperation speaks of another tacit supranational regional agenda for cultural policy, responding to forces of globalisation. So despite skipping scales, we feel confident that our approach sheds new light on cultural policy and cultural policy research, providing novel insights into this admittedly heterogeneous landscape.

READING *CULTURAL POLICY*

We hope, ultimately, that this book encourages the continued practices of getting to know and intervening in cultural policy. We will end this introduction by briefly summarising each chapter, offering a sketch map of what lies ahead. In the next chapter, we turn our attention to the 'culture' of cultural policy. This chapter explores the remit of cultural policy, analysing which cultural forms and practices have traditionally been considered the responsibility of cultural policy and which have not. It explores the debates about high/low, traditional or popular culture and, by looking at the influence of cultural studies on cultural policy debates, examines the battles for legitimacy and support for popular or subcultural forms and practices. It also looks at how cultural activities have been classified and understood over time, introducing notions such as the cultural industries, the creative economy and the creative industries. Finally, it considers how cultural consumption has been conceptualised and assessed from the standpoint of cultural policy, drawing on discussions of cultural capital.

The aim of Chapter 3 is to understand cultural policy as a form of public policy, and to explore what that means for our analyses of cultural policy. The chapter outlines debates within the emerging field of cultural policy studies and discusses the 'torn halves' of critical and applied work. It explores the question of who makes cultural policy – a question whose answer is more complicated than might first appear. It also considers the question of how cultural policy gets made. It sketches the relationship between disciplinary location and the methods and approaches used to conduct academic research into cultural policy and considers forms of research that are used within cultural policy making. Certain examples – such as the UK's local cultural strategies – are examined closely in order to show the many different ways we need to think about cultural policy: as text, as discourse, as process and as practice. Drawing on previous research to exemplify each approach, the chapter maps how different methodological approaches have been used to analyse cultural policy. Finally, it examines research into policy mobility, looking at how, where and why cultural policies travel.

Chapter 4 looks at cultural policy in the city, which it argues has perhaps been the prime site for policy innovation in the last 30 years. Having considered why the city has become so important in this respect, the chapter considers a variety of ways in which urban policymakers have sought to use culture for policy agendas ranging from economic development to quality of life and from city branding to regeneration. It also asks what is at stake and what is at risk in this instrumental use of culture and considers both the failings of contemporary cultural policies, particularly in terms of gentrification, as well as resistance to policy interventions, and attempts to develop more sustainable cultural landscapes within our cities.

The scale of the nation, of national government, might seem like the most prominent and obvious scale for cultural policy analysis. However, many national governments have displayed considerable ambivalence towards direct management of the arts and culture, and academics working at the national scale have defined various different orientations towards cultural policy on the part of the nation-state, from direct intervention to a distinctly hands-off (or arm's-length) approach. In Chapter 5 we critically review these attempts to produce a typology of national cultural policy approaches and outline studies of both specific countries and of cross-national comparison. The chapter also considers the uses of culture by national governments and nation-states, and the interplay between party politics and cultural policy at national level, before looking 'beyond' the nation at subnational and supranational cultural policy. Using examples from countries around the world, the chapter provides a critical overview of debates about the contested relationship between nation, state and culture.

The internationalisation of the world economy provides a fundamental context for the production, consumption and distribution of cultural products, yet cultural policy has until recently failed to keep pace with these developments. Chapter 6 considers what some regard as an overlooked area of research on cultural policy: the question of international cultural policy. It considers issues such as cultural trade, diplomacy, diversity and the role of culture in economic and social development, particularly in the Global South. In so doing it argues that while the agencies of international cultural policy – UNESCO, WIPO, UNCTAD and so on – may seem remote from the concerns of the average cultural producer or consumer, their activities increasingly shape the cultural (and cultural policy) environment. This chapter ends with a brief conclusion, summarising the main issues raised throughout *Cultural Policy*.

NOTES

1 See www.leeds.gov.uk/museumsandgalleries/Pages/leedsartgallery/Picture-Lending. aspx (accessed 10 March 2014).

REFERENCES AND FURTHER READING

Allen, J., Massey, D., Cochrane, A., Charlesworth, J., Court, G., Henry, N. and Sarre, P. (1998) *Rethinking the Region*, London: Routledge.

Belfiore, E. (2004) 'Auditing culture: the subsidised cultural sector in the New Public Management', *International Journal of Cultural Policy*, 10(2): 183–202.

Bell, D. and Valentine, G. (1997) *Consuming Geographies: We are Where we Eat*, London: Routledge.

Bennett, T. (1995) *The Birth of the Museum: History, Theory, Politics*, London: Routledge.

——(1998) *Culture: a Reformer's Science*, London: Sage.

Bourdieu, P. (1984) *Distinction: a Social Critique of the Judgment of Taste*, Harvard MA: Harvard University Press.

Cunningham, S. (2009). 'Trojan horse or Rorschach blot? Creative industries discourse around the world'. *International Journal of Cultural Policy*, 15(4), 375–86.

Eurobarometer (2013) *Cultural Access and Participation*, Special Report 399. Available at http://ec.europa.eu/public_opinion/archives/ebs/ebs_399_en.pdf (accessed 15/12/13).

Gray, C. (2000) *The Politics of the Arts in Britain*, Basingstoke: Macmillan.

——(2010) 'Analysing cultural policy: incorrigibly plural or ontologically incompatible?' *International Journal of Cultural Policy*, 16(2): 215–30.

Häring, N. and Douglas, N. (2012) *Economists and the Powerful: Convenient Theories, Distorted Facts, Ample Rewards*, London: Anthem Press.

Herod, A. (2010) *Scale*, London: Routledge.

McCann, E. and Ward, K. (2011) 'Urban assemblages: territories, relations, practices, and power', in E. McCann and K. Ward (eds) *Mobile Urbanism: Cities and Policymaking in the Global Age*, Minneapolis MN: University of Minnesota Press.

Miller, T. and Yudice, G. (2002) *Cultural Policy*, London: Sage.

Mirowski, P. (2013) *Never Let a Serious Crisis Go to Waste: How Neoliberalism Survived the Financial Meltdown*, London: Verso.

O'Brien, D. (2013) *Cultural Policy: Management, Value and Modernity in the Creative Industries*, London: Routledge.

O'Brien, D. and Miles, S. (2010) 'Cultural policy as rhetoric and reality: a comparative analysis of policy making in the peripheral north of England', *Cultural Trends*, 19(1): 3–13.

Painter, C. (ed.) (2002) *Contemporary Art and the Home*, Oxford: Berg.

Turner, A. (2012) *Economics after the Crisis: Objectives and Means*, Cambridge MA: MIT Press.

Turner, G. (2014) 'Culture, politics and the cultural industries: reviving a critical agenda', in K. Oakley and J. O'Connor (eds) *The Routledge Companion to the Cultural Industries*, London: Routledge

UNESCO (2013) *The Creative Economy Report: Widening Local Development Pathways*, New York: UNESCO.

Volkering, M. (2001) 'From Cool Britannia to Hot Nation: "creative industries" policies in Europe, Canada and New Zealand', *Cultural Policy*, 7(3): 437–55.

2

THE CULTURE OF CULTURAL POLICY

DEFINING CULTURE

The first task facing the analyst of cultural policy is to understand what forms of culture fall within the remit of public policy and why. This is not, as sometimes assumed, the same as understanding what the term 'culture' means. Whether we take a broad view of culture as encompassing a whole way of life or a narrower one, referring to artistic activities alone, we can come to understand that not all cultural activities are likely to be the subject of cultural policy in the same fashion. The way the state interacts with, supports, represses or regulates different cultural forms is highly selective and contingent, and it is the task of this chapter to analyse how the 'culture' of cultural policy is determined.

The definition of culture in most of the ways we currently use the term emerged in the nineteenth century through two contrasting approaches: culture as a set of artistic practices or products, and culture as an anthropological signifying system marking human society off from nature. In the first sense, associated with Victorian thinkers such as Mathew Arnold, culture is an idealised practice to which humans can and should aspire; it represents our better selves and can help us to re-think and indeed remake our world. Despite being published in the 1860s,[1] these ideas of Arnold's – about the civilising nature of art – continue to influence cultural policy and are part of its rationale over a century and a half later. The second, anthropological sense of the term culture, which can include ways of eating, dressing or worshipping, is generally not part of the remit of cultural policy in much of Europe and North and South America and societies such as Canada and Australia. In these cases, cultural policy tends to confine itself to culture in the sense of artistic activities; though what counts as artistic can be very broad and is deeply contested.

The anthropological sense of culture – as a way of life – has however remained influential, both in the discourse of 'development,' particularly as applied in post-colonial societies in the Global South, and as part of the rethinking of 'culture' that has taken place, partly under the influence of cultural studies. What is referred to as 'intangible cultural heritage', a broad group of phenomena which includes oral traditions and languages, rituals and even spiritual beliefs, is recognised in UNESCO's framework for culture (see Chapter 6). Throughout the twentieth century and particularly since the 1940s, the story of cultural policy has been one of steady movement from a narrow focus on the high arts to one which encompasses a broader range of cultural practices, though it remains unlikely to cover all 'ways of life'.

The issues raised by using a very broad definition of culture as way of life is, as various commentators point out (Gray 2010; Hesmondhalgh 2005; Looseley 1995; McGuigan 1996), that it is difficult to know where 'culture' ends and 'everything else' begins. This is difficult from an analytical point of view, but even more so from the point of view of public policy, which tends to require a bounded set of activities and understandings with which to engage. For the most part, what we understand by the culture of cultural policy is, as Storey (2006: 2) puts it, 'the texts and practices whose principle function is to signify, to produce or to be the occasion for the production of meaning'.

Although both state and religious patronage of 'artistic activities' has a long history, debates about the culture of cultural policy are of somewhat more recent derivation. The years immediately after the Second World War saw the state in many European countries not only use public money in the form of tax revenues to support culture for the first time, but also articulate its own grounds for so doing. When the British Arts Council was established in 1946, its purpose was described by the economist and guiding spirit John Maynard Keynes as:

> to stimulate, comfort and support any societies or bodies brought together on private or local initiative, which are striving with serious purpose and a reasonable prospect of success to present for public enjoyment the arts of drama, music and painting.
>
> (Keynes 1982: 368)

As Raymond Williams ([1981b] 1989) has pointed out, this left out not only literature but also film, photography, radio and television. The omission of the media industries from the Arts Council's remit remains to this day, with occasional exceptions; but in other respects Keynes' vision of the Council was extremely far-sighted. Once material needs had been met, Keynes was convinced that

> New work will spring up more abundantly in unexpected quarters and in unforeseen shapes when there is a universal opportunity for contact with traditional and contemporary arts in the noblest forms.
>
> (Keynes 1945, quoted in Williams [1981b] 1989: 22)

The need to recognise and support emerging cultural forms was thus part of the British Arts Council's remit from its earliest days, though its success in doing this could be described as mixed. Many of the most heated debates within cultural policy over the decades from the 1940s onwards have been those concerning that border between culture as art and culture as a way of life. The degree to which popular culture is the remit of cultural policy was, and remains, one of the core debates in this field, and popular culture is sometimes seen to include more of the 'way of life' activities – watching TV, clubbing, posting on Facebook – than traditional or elite culture does.

As cultural policy has sought to engage with a wider range of artistic activities – particularly popular cultural ones – it has often been accused of drifting towards the anthropological meaning, as it was in France under the Mitterand regime (Looseley 1995). This is particularly the case when policymakers are seeking to promote a relationship between cultural activities and other public policy goals or use culture to address particular social concerns such as unemployment or community relations (Looseley 1995).

A recent document from Lambeth Council in South London illustrates this point. *Wellbeing through Culture: Developing a Cultural Commissioning Strategy for Lambeth* (Lambeth 2010) considers how local government might promote wellbeing, a current concern of many Western governments (Stiglitz *et al.* 2009), via its purported link with cultural activities. In the document, culture is at one point defined as 'things to do and places to go' (Lambeth 2010:10), and these 'things and places' include hotels, cafes, sports facilities and tourism. Yet is such a broad definition satisfying, either analytically or practically?

From an analytic point of view, it is clear that eating in restaurants is a cultural activity (Beriss and Sutton 2007); we do not do it because we are hungry (though we may be) and the type of foods, services and expected behaviours are deeply imbued with symbolic meaning. But while we don't eat in restaurants *merely* to assuage hunger, we don't do so primarily to engage with these meanings either. If we follow the restaurant meal with a trip to the cinema, the difference is reasonably clear. Eating has multiple functions, one of which is to feed us, while watching a film is 'the main purpose and even an end in itself' (McGuigan 2004: 23).

Thus, while cultural policy primarily concerns itself with artistic forms of culture, it increasingly feels the need to articulate these with broader sets of activities, partly as way of achieving wider (not simply cultural) goals. In fact, the drift of public policy-making in recent decades has been to more 'decentred' formation (Bevir and Rhodes 2003), and cultural policy is no exception. Cultural activities in recent decades have arguably been more affected by 'non-cultural' policies such as urban planning, education or immigration policy than by what we might once have conceived of as 'policy for the arts'. Those policies are therefore made in economic ministries and urban planners' offices, in trade negotiations and legal arguments about intellectual property, not just in cultural ministries – and a student of cultural policy needs to be aware of these wider debates if she is to make sense of policy directions.

As Bennett (1998) has argued, however, we should not confuse the fact that cultural policy is now made by more policy actors than it was in the past, with the argument that culture, or indeed cultural policy, is becoming more democratic. While cultural practices have become more prominent within a wide range of policy discussions, the ownership and control of cultural assets has become more concentrated (Hesmondhalgh 2005). And while governments have expanded the range of cultural activities deemed worthy of support, the purpose of including certain types of culture and not others remains a highly normative one, whether the aim is to remake citizens through engagement with Beethoven or through engagement with community media in Lambeth.

A related debate is the degree to which cultural policy should encourage citizens to take part in particular sorts of activities (going to the theatre or a concert, for example) or should simply start from learning what people do in their spare time, and support those activities. Should cultural policy start from the view that some cultural activities are better for us than others, which many would argue has been its traditional role? Or should it simply try to vary our cultural diet, recognising that we are more likely to come across contemporary popular music in the ordinary course of life than we are to encounter jazz or classical music? Or should it seek to support no particular cultural forms at all but simply support our consumer preferences?

HIGH, LOW AND EVERYTHING IN-BETWEEN

Arguing that cultural policy primarily engages with artistic forms of culture still does not tell us why certain artistic activities have been supported in the past and others have not. Lewis and Miller (2003: 3) summarise a common point of view when they argue that those practices which do fall within the remit of cultural policy are, 'on the whole, a culture chosen and defined by cultural elites, for an audience with the requisite cultural capital'. Thus, what is sometimes called 'high' or traditional culture – for example, classical music, opera, ballet and museums – tends to account for the bulk of public cultural spending in most countries, with subsidy generally inversely proportional to public consumption (Looseley 1995). The rationales for these inclusions will have differed over time, yet despite this it is striking how resistant the composition of art forms, indeed of arts institutions that form the bulk of publicly funded culture, has been to change. To take one obvious example, the Royal Opera House, the UK's primary opera company, has accounted for the single largest institutional Arts Council funding every year from 1946 to the present day.

This is not to suggest that cultural policy has not played a role in supporting other cultural practices, particularly the growth of the mass media. Britain's foremost cultural institution – the BBC – is the creation of public policy and has been largely publicly funded, via a hypothecated tax known as the licence fee, for its entire life. Indeed, one of the casualties of the separation of cultural from media policy, in both practice and academic study (see Chapter 1), has been the failure to explain how cultural policy influences the whole of our cultural life, not just the arts on one hand or the media on the other. Nevertheless, it remains the case that while the growth of the commercial media industries has outstripped that of any other cultural form in the past century – not merely economically, but culturally – cultural policy has often seemed to concern itself primarily with a defensive role, supporting non-market high culture against encroachment from the mass market.

In an essay written in 1981, Raymond Williams writes of four different ways in which the objectives of cultural policy may be understood:

state patronage of fine arts;
pump-priming;
intervention in the market;
expanding and changing popular culture.
(Williams [1981b] 1989)

An analysis of the policies of most European countries, as well as countries like Australia or Canada, would suggest that the two first aims, patronage of the arts and some funding for production, have been the primary activities in most cases (Upchurch 2004). Intervention in the market was the goal of those who favoured a 'cultural industries' approach to policy (see section below), though many would question the degree to which this has ever been properly realised. For Williams ([1981b] 1989: 148), 'expanding and changing popular culture' was the only really legitimate grounds on which to 'raise money for the arts from the general revenue'. It is notable that Williams talks about *expanding and changing* popular culture, however, not simply funding people's access to it, which he assumed would take place through the market. For Williams, popular culture had the same potential to produce great work as other forms of culture, but this may require intervention; he was not simply celebrating popular culture as it currently existed. Nonetheless, it seemed reasonable to assert that, as the majority of people were paying for cultural spending via their taxes, they may expect to see more of the kinds of culture they enjoy being supported.

Yet if defining culture is difficult, defining popular culture is by no means easy. Often confused with mass culture (Adorno 1991) or commercial culture (Cowen 1998), one obvious meaning of the term is something which is popular and enjoyed by large numbers of people. This is clearly part of the story, but even a short reflection would suggest that the importance of subcultures within popular culture, particularly in popular music, means that large numbers alone cannot define it (Hebdige 1979).

Another way to identify popular culture is by comparison with its 'other': the notion of high or traditional culture. To do so requires a degree of historical ignorance, however. Both Shakespeare and Dickens would be seen as part of the high culture canon today, yet both were regarded as popular entertainers by contemporaries. Film as a medium started much as videogames did – regarded generally as a set of technical gizmos which entertained but did not enlighten – yet over the course of the twentieth century what one might call a film canon has arisen which would see some films attaining the status of art. These are sometimes referred to as art house films, by directors such as Tarkovsky or Kurosawa, but also include popular classics such as *Singin' in the Rain* (Wollen 2012) and *Psycho.* Another meaning is to see popular culture as the culture of the people, occasionally viewed as linked to traditional or folk culture, but more often taken to mean the culture that most people enjoy and produce in their everyday lives (MacDonald 2003). It was in this sense that Williams described culture as 'ordinary' (Williams 1958).

The degree to which popular culture means commercial culture has been (and remains) contested, yet this link has been used for many years to argue against public support for popular cultural activities. The argument is that the normal operations of the market will produce enough high-quality popular fiction, films, TV programmes and popular music, so that no intervention beyond competition law is required (Cowen 1998). Within media policy however, the reality of public service broadcasting, at least in many European countries, has always posed a clear practical challenge to such as an idea. The BBC, publicly funded and central to the UK's cultural establishment, has been in the business of providing popular entertainment alongside news, documentary and children's programmes since its initiation. Other agencies, the arts councils in particular, but also film funding bodies and heritage organisations have, in the decades since the middle of the twentieth century, gradually broadened their funding to support more popular cultural activities, though rarely without controversy. Whether it was the UK National Trust's[2] decision to purchase and preserve the childhood home of Beatles John Lennon and Paul McCartney or the UK Film Council's funding of popular comedies, public cultural agencies consistently grapple with how to support Keynes' 'unforeseen shapes' of popular cultural work (Keynes 1945, in Williams [1981] 1989).

One of the difficulties is deciding what elements of contemporary popular culture are worth supporting without the benefit of hindsight. Even advocates of a purely market-based approach to cultural production concede that only a portion of any period's cultural output will stand the famous 'test of time' (Cowen 1998). One of the favourite games of the annual Oscar awards for best film is marvelling at the fact that John Ford's sentimental *How Green was*

My Valley was preferred over *Citizen Kane* in 1941, or *Rocky* over Sydney Lumet's *Network* in 1976. The status of the Beatles or Bob Dylan may be assured, but intervening in current popular music production is difficult: choices have to be made, sometimes without any help from what Williams (1973: 44) called the 'culture of the selective tradition'.

A crude argument, sometimes made by those who fear that the state's engagement with popular culture is a case of 'dumbing down', is to state that that all 'judgement' has been abandoned or that while judgements are frequently made in high culture, popular culture is a sort of aesthetic free-for-all, where people 'like what they like' and don't want to be told otherwise (Jenkins 2012). Yet as Justin O'Connor has noted,

> those engaged with popular culture constantly make distinctions. This has always been so in the realm of fashion, of various 'in crowds', cliques, scenes, gangs, subcultures – the whole gamut of popular culture deals in discriminations and exclusions.
>
> (O'Connor 2004: 64)

Even within popular culture therefore, selections are made, though by whom and according to what criteria is sometimes difficult to determine. As children of the 1970s we have often been mystified by a media class which seems, through popular television programmes, to present a decade consisting entirely of strikes, glam rock and Space Hoppers (Sandbrook 2012), while we can also recall the growth of feminism, gay rights, the anti-nuclear movement and the Velvet Underground (Beckett 2010). So we always need to be careful when thinking about who forms a 'cultural elite' and thus who does the selecting at any particular time. Cultural elites can come in various shapes and sizes, and when it comes to popular culture, market-based or commercial elites are generally more powerful than the image of a public sector 'cultural elite' making decisions about what gets funded and what does not.

Thus, the inclusion of popular cultural practices within mainstream cultural policy posed and still poses particular challenges for the policymaker. By the 1980s it was no longer possible to argue that the culture which was worthy of support needed to be protected from the market; the strength of the commercial cultural industries and the growth of mass media which could bring most of them into people's homes meant that, for the majority of the population, culture *is* commercial culture. If cultural policy was to retain any legitimacy, it needed to find ways of intervening 'in and through the market' (Garnham 1987).

THE CULTURAL INDUSTRIES DEBATE

The term 'cultural industries', for many the preferred way to describe the core media and cultural sectors (Hesmondhalgh 2002), comes loaded with a particular set of historical and intellectual baggage, which needs unpacking a little before we can discuss its meaning within cultural policy. The term 'culture industry' is most readily associated with Marxist philosophers Theodore Adorno and Max Horkheimer, and particularly with their work *Dialectic of Enlightenment* ([1947] 2002) which was written in the United States during their exile from Nazi Germany. As befits the Frankfurt School tradition from which it springs, the book takes a critical (indeed pessimistic) view of what had happened to culture under conditions of industrial capitalism. For Adorno and Horkheimer, art, which was once able to offer a critique of society, had now been so thoroughly subsumed by the economy – turned into an industry – that any possibility of critique was lost (Adorno 1991). Art could no longer suggest a better future to us because it had become part and parcel of capitalism itself. It was not there to show audiences a different sort of society but to make them accept the one they had. Indeed, what could be presented as greater consumer choice in the proliferation of cultural products was in fact standardised production with only minor differences, 'where something is provided for all, so that none may escape' (Adorno and Horkheimer [1947] 2002: 351).

The relationship between political and aesthetic revolution – the links between modernism and the *avant garde* – had been central to left-wing thought since at least the mid-nineteenth century. For Adorno and Horkheimer, the seeming collapse of the eman-cipatory possibilities of art was cause for despair. But, as Justin

O'Connor (2010) has argued, Adorno should not therefore be thought of simply as a conservative critic of mass culture; in drawing attention to the industrialisation of cultural production, his work laid the foundation for other thinkers, and also policymakers, to seek to understand the role of culture in modern capitalist democracies. Adorno asked if there was any role for culture outside or beyond its role in economic production and hence in its profit-making forms. It is a question that has become more, not less, relevant as time has gone on.

Adorno's account of the culture industry resonated with post-war concerns, particularly in Europe, about the dominance of mass, industrial or 'Americanised' culture (Hoggart 1957), and the wish to protect the European cultural tradition against these threats (see Chapter 6 for further discussion). However, while critically engaging with Adorno and Horkheimer's work, other writers, particularly Bernard Miege (1989), sought to develop its insights in a way that reflected both the politics of the post-1960s, with its stress on the rights of hitherto marginalised groups, and the growing understanding of the complexities of industrialised cultural production.

If the period since the 1950s has seen a general extension of those cultural forms deemed worthy of public support, the 1970s and 1980s witnessed a much more radical change in the idea of what cultural policy should encompass. Across Western Europe, leftist urban governments had sought to develop policies that moved away from the traditional arm's-length support for the high arts, in favour of a more consciously politicised stance (Bianchini 1987). This was linked to a whole range of post-1968 social movements – environmentalism, feminism, gay and ethnic minority activism – all of whom had associated cultural arguments, often about the rediscovery of hitherto suppressed arts forms and artists. Embracing this meant that policy, at least at the urban if not the national level, moved from a traditional high arts argument to one that embraced particular aspects of popular culture, particularly those associated with 'alternative' culture, such as fanzines, independent film makers, radical publishers and so on (Bianchini 1987).

In doing so, it recognised firstly that the commodification of culture was a much more messy and ambivalent process than

Horkheimer and Adorno had allowed for, and secondly that the manipulation of audience response to products – the idea of the cultural dupe passively consuming American popular culture – could not be sustained. The cultural industry was by no means as in control of the product or of the market as it might appear, and the industrialisation of cultural production opened up new possible forms of meaning, even while it appeared to close down others. Far from being able to predict consumer responses to cultural products, most producers had little or no idea of what would sell. And thirdly, those producers involved in the systems of mass production – from filmmakers to popular musicians – had their own concerns about autonomy, their own messages to convey and their own political views – sometimes at odds with those who owned the firms that paid them.

Yet those thinkers who sought to translate the cultural industries idea into public policy were not simply content with the culture that markets produced, but instead were influenced by Williams' argument about the need to expand and change popular culture. As Hesmondhalgh (2012: 167) puts it, 'the aim was not to celebrate commercial production, but simply to recognise its centrality in modern culture'. In France for example, concerns about the 'Americanisation' of national culture had a long history and led to a series of measures under the Mitterrand government of the 1980s, including a quota system for the showing of French films, both at the cinema and on television (Looseley 1995). But beyond what was sometimes criticised as simply cultural nationalism, French policy was beginning to recognise 'that the relationship between culture and the economy was dialectical and therefore potentially positive' (Looseley 1995: 80).

In Britain, these ideas witnessed perhaps their clearest expression in the case of London during the period 1983–6, in what is generally referred to as the 'cultural industries' strategy of the Greater London Council (GLC). This went beyond merely seeking to extend the remit of existing cultural policy to forms of popular culture, and argued that the mechanisms by which such policies might be enacted also needed to change. The GLC's Industry and Employment Committee under the influence of figures like Robin Murray and academic Nick Garnham, drawing on Miege's work in France, had developed approaches to the cultural industries which sought to break down distinctions between subsidised and commercial culture. As most people's cultural consumption was hugely shaped by market forces, cultural policy needed to take account of this, they argued, and could thus include public investments in commercial enterprises such as recording studios, publishing houses and magazines, and even commercial sports organisations (Garnham 1990). Any analysis of the market for cultural products, Garnham argued, suggested that cultural policy should focus on distribution, including subsidising audience and market research for small cultural businesses, in an attempt to help foster self-sufficiency and offer a genuine alternative to the current commercial gatekeepers. In this way, culture did not need to be defended from the market, but it might need to be supported *within* the market, providing an alternative which could reaffirm the critical role of culture, which Adorno feared had been extinguished.

Publicly funding alternative distribution channels, particularly in terms of broadcasting, was considered by the GLC, but as with many of its cultural industry policies, these remained ideas rather than practical interventions. The GLC was abolished in 1986 by the then-Conservative national government before most of its cultural policies saw the light of day; however, they remain highly influential. The belief in the economic importance of the cultural sectors, particularly but not only the media, had taken root and was to shift the terrain of cultural policy towards a more prominent, if problematic, relationship with notions of economic competiveness and growth. Similarly, the idea of local, particularly urban, cultural strategies that combined funding for new cultural infrastructure with economic development of the cultural sectors, was to be replicated in cities across the globe (see Chapter 5). And the idea that the distinction between subsidised 'high' culture and commercial popular culture was a hard-and-fast one was fatally weakened. What was lost in subsequent versions of this policy, however, was the idea of *critical engagement* with markets, the role of the state as countering and occasionally subverting market forces. Future developments of the cultural industries notion would have quite a different political complexion.

THE CREATIVE INDUSTRIES

Unlike many of the terms we have examined so far – 'culture', 'popular culture', 'the arts' – the creative industries as a notion has a clear beginning, the formation of the Creative Industries Taskforce in the UK in 1997, and a relatively clear (if highly problematic) definition:

> those industries which have their origin in individual creativity, skill and talent and which have a potential for wealth and job creation through the generation and exploitation of intellectual property.
>
> (DCMS 2001: 4)

Established by the incoming British Labour government in 1997, the Creative Industries Taskforce set about measuring and mapping what it defined as the 13 creative industry sectors (see Figure 2.1 below). Attempts to quantity the growing economic importance of the cultural industries has been underway for some time in the UK and elsewhere (Myerscough 1998). But while large commercial organisations and indeed major public cultural institutions were easy enough to count for statistical purposes, the fact was that much cultural production was due to the work of small firms and self-employed or freelance labour. For a new cultural ministry, keen to persuade other government departments, particularly the finance ministry (Treasury) of the importance of the cultural sectors, it was thought vital to demonstrate just how significant an economic force cultural production was becoming. The creative industries idea thus extended the definition of the cultural sectors beyond the traditional arts and media and into the creative services – namely, design, architecture and advertising (NESTA 2006).

Table 2.1 UK creative industries

Advertising	Music
Architecture	Performing arts
Arts and antiques	Publishing
Crafts	Software and computer services
Design	Television and radio
Designer fashion	Interactive leisure software
Film	

Source: Department of Culture, Media and Sport

The change of terminology, from cultural to creative industries, was not without significance and has been much commented on in the academic literature (Garnham 2005; Hesmondhalgh 2008; O'Connor 2007). The inclusion of service industries like advertising and design clearly moved the remit beyond what we have referred to above as the cultural industries. In part this was pragmatic, as was the contentious inclusion of 'software' as a creative industry. Broadening the definition in this way and with the calculations taking place in the late 1990s, in the period proceeding what became known as the 'dot com' boom, the Creative Industries Taskforce was able to claim that creative industries jobs accounted for nearly 8 per cent of the UK economy and, more importantly, they were growing at a faster rate than most other economic sectors (Oakley 2014).

This helped to establish a link between the cultural sectors and economic growth that has formed the basis of almost every policy document written on the creative industries since (van Heur 2008). Such an approach has had global appeal; as Stuart Cunningham (2009: 376) has commented, 'even the sternest critic of the creative industries idea would concede that it has had a remarkable take-up across many parts of the world'. For Cunningham this is a beneficial outcome of the protean nature of the creative industries idea, which allows governments of various stripes and in various political settlements to fashion a role for culture that speaks to their own desire for economic development. And indeed there is some variation in the use of their term (now often broadened to the confusing 'cultural and creative industries'), which means that while the UK includes fashion in its creative industry sectors but not museums, France includes museums but – perhaps surprisingly – not fashion (Newbigin 2010).

The change in terminology from cultural to creative also has significant political implications, signalling a retreat from the leftist politics that directed many local government interventions in the cultural sector, notably that of the GLC in London. Underlying these approaches had been a desire not simply to intervene in the market but also to shape it, to challenge the dominance of large commercial interests in both the production and the distribution of cultural products in favour of a broader and more democratic cultural marketplace. The creative industries approach, while keen on supporting the production of cultural products – and particularly on stimulating the development of small cultural businesses – was significantly less keen on intervening in wider market structures. In line with the neoliberal dominance of politics at the time, the role of policy was to focus on the supply side – and a variety of interventions were indeed developed to help small firms, but not to challenge the vested commercial interests that dominated and still dominate cultural production and distribution.

Thus, the global success of the creative industries as an idea owes as much to the fact that it speaks to prevailing political agendas as it does to its use of empirical evidence or articulation of sources of economic growth. The creative industries are growing worldwide, in some cases faster than the rest of the economy, particularly as at the time of writing we are in a prolonged economic slump. But some of the more enthusiastic claims of these industries have not been borne out. While worldwide growth is evident (UNESCO 2013), there are wide differences across national and regional areas and between cultural activities. Those subsectors that benefit from public subsidy – notably the performing arts and heritage – have seen contraction, particularly in Europe, while what is sometimes called 'old' media – newspapers, the music industry, film – are struggling to find new business models as the growth of digital technology threatens existing revenues (Doyle 2013).

THE CREATIVE OR CULTURAL ECONOMY?

Despite the success of the creative industries model, therefore, the terminology is far from settled and a number of other terms continue to co-exist (see UNESCO 2013: 19–25 for a useful discussion). In almost all cases these terms are not neutral and carry a particular ideological message; indeed, the debate about 'cultural' or 'creative' industries is currently being enacted in a new form in the debate about creative or cultural economy.

The term 'creative economy' (currently preferred by UNESCO and other international agencies) represents yet another change in meaning rather than just terminology. It seeks to capture the impact of the cultural industries in terms of the technologies they help create or the consumer markets they help shape – and therefore in the wider economy, beyond culture itself. It is less concerned with the growth of the cultural sectors themselves and more about how their growth can drive wider economic growth. There are different schools of thought about the relationship between culture and the wider economy and as yet no dominant account of how this relationship works has emerged.

One approach is what is sometimes called the 'culturisation' thesis: the argument that cultural objects themselves proliferate in a variety of forms, 'as information, as communications, as branded products, as media products, as transport and leisure services, cultural entities are no longer the exception: they are the rule' (Lash and Lury 2007: 8), and are therefore no longer primarily symbolic. However, these ideas, coming as they do from a critical social science tradition, have been less influential on policy thinking than ideas more informed by business or economics, which tend to promote the links between culture and the wider economy rather than analyse them.

Another series of attempts to model the relationship of the creative and cultural sectors to the rest of the economy has been to use cultural economist David Throsby's 'concentric circle' model of the cultural sectors (Throsby 2010), which describes the creative arts as the source and generator of ideas that are later picked up by other cultural industries such as the media (see for example, Andari *et al.* 2007; UNESCO 2013). While Throsby was keen to investigate what he sees as the 'core' arts and the wider commercial cultural industries, in part as a way of understanding the relationship between public subsidy and the wider economy, other interpretations of this work in a policy context have sought to extend the notion of 'expressive value' beyond the cultural and creative industries and firmly into those areas which produce non-cultural outputs, such as the Dyson vacuum cleaner (Andari *et al.* 2007).

Other work claims that 'human capital' is the mechanism of transmission; in essence that there are more people working in creative occupations in the wider economy than in the cultural sectors (Higgs *et al.* 2008; NESTA 2013). Design is often seen as crucial for this argument as there are generally more designers working outside the creative industries (in manufacturing, for example) than there are within them (for example, in design consultancies). But attempts to broaden this argument beyond design are less convincing as this depends on accepting the notion that town planners, software professionals and library assistants are 'creative workers', which stretches the definition way beyond any reasonably cultural occupation and therefore turns into a slightly circular argument. On what basis are these 'creative occupations' creative? Is it because many of them are cultural occupations such as dance, acting or photography? In which case why include town planning, which is not an explicitly cultural activity? And if 'creative' simply means 'works with new ideas' or some such, why include musicians but not research chemists?

The general direction of such debates is to move what we might call 'creative economy' policies further away from concern with cultural and artistic consumption and production and more towards generalised innovation policy. As such, it reopens the gap between 'culture' and 'the economy' that cultural industries advocates were trying to close from the 1980s onwards. The absence of a critical politics of culture, signalled by the move to 'creative industries' terminology, is here taken a step further; the beneficial nature of economic growth as a purpose for policy is generally unquestioned and any notion of an oppositional stance for culture – as something which sits outside mainstream society – is firmly resisted. Culture and commerce in this view are not in any sort of historical tension or dynamic but are happily joined.

A report published by NESTA in the UK in 2013 seeks to redefine the creative industries as 'those sectors which specialise in the use of creative talent for commercial purposes' (NESTA 2013: 13). This suggest that non-commercial cultural production – in the voluntary and public sectors, for example – is not to be included in the definition of the creative industries and the purpose of such activities is entirely commercial, with no reference to social, political or cultural motivations. As such, cultural policy would return to a concern primarily with the subsidised arts, while innovation policy would be all that was needed to regulate and support much of popular culture. The attempt to develop policies that recognise how culture is shaped by the market and what needs to be done in order to prevent concentrations of market power from distorting cultural production and consumption would be at an end.

As we discuss in Chapter 6, other definitions of the 'creative economy' are being formulated, particularly in transnational organisations such as UNESCO. Adding to the confusion, these come under the heading of 'cultural economy' and take a very different approach, much less focussed on the purely commercial aspects of culture. This tradition argues that our cultural under-standings (in the broadest anthropological sense of this term) are what shape our understanding of society, including what we under-stand as 'the economy' (Amin and Thrift 2004). Thus, culture can help us to rethink what we want from 'the economy', whether that is simply more consumer goods and services or whether a different set of values and rationales is implied. As Chris Gibson puts it, for him the term cultural economy 'resonates well with the imminent requirement that we question current, unsustainable economic practices – requiring, I would argue, a bolder sense of normative critique of the rightness/wrongness of forms of production and commoditisation' (Gibson 2011: 6).

In this sense it may be that we are seeing two very different approaches to policy development for the cultural industries. One is very strongly focussed on economic growth under what one might call the current growth model; the other stresses the limits of economic growth as the goal of cultural or indeed any public policy. This opposition between conservative and radical, or left and right, approaches to cultural policy is not new but has played out in different ways at different historical junctures. At the same time, big questions remain about how cultural consumption has changed over this period and what role remains for public policy in shaping that.

CONSUMING HIGH AND LOW

Who gets to consume culture and under what conditions have always been important question for cultural policymakers. While the 'cultural industries' policy moment sought to recognise that most people's cultural consumption came via the market rather than public subsidy and therefore that policies to broaden and democratise cultural consumption needed to tackle the market, subsequent developments under the creative industries/economy banner have moved away from this idea and focussed more on the relationship between cultural production and economic growth. So it is worth asking what has happened to cultural consumption in this period? As the cultural industries – now joined by a host of Internet and digital industries – have become a larger part of the economy, does policy still need to concern itself with access to culture? And what types of culture does it concern itself with?

The social stratification of cultural consumption – the finding that, broadly speaking, income, class and social status are correlated with cultural consumption – has been recognised for some time. Much of the research in this area is associated with, or derives from, the work of French sociologist Pierre Bourdieu (e.g. Bourdieu 1984), who analysed cultural consumption as part of what he termed 'cultural capital', the idea that certain kinds of cultural taste and knowledge – generally high culture – formed a sort of asset which individuals could use to not only segment their place in society but, by passing it on to their children (for example, through private music or ballet lessons) make it central to the reproduction of a class-divided society. Unlike some uses of the term 'cultural capital', particularly in policy documents, where it often seems to mean simply a knowledge of culture which all can benefit from, Bourdieu's sense of cultural capital was as a means by which class conflict took place, with the dominant class in society using particular forms of cultural consumption as a means to maintain status difference.

Cultural policymakers, while not generally engaging with the full force of Bourdieu's social critique, have used his insights, particularly about the inter-generational transmission of cultural knowledge, to argue for the importance of education – and cultural education in particular – in developing the habits of cultural consumption in children. Even good public education systems find it difficult to combat inequality in access to cultural participation in childhood. Children from middle-class families are more likely to make trips to the theatre, museum or concert hall, in addition to visits organised by their school, than children from poorer backgrounds (Bennett *et al.* 2009). But the argument for the importance of school-based cultural activities in developing the habits of both cultural consumption and production has enabled cultural advocates to lobby for funds from (generally larger) public education budgets. There is some evidence that sustained exposure to forms of cultural participation and consumption in school can help children from all backgrounds in areas ranging from improved self-confidence to better communication skills (Bamford 2006). However, despite this evidence, and perhaps because the evidence that cultural exposure can lead to better *exam* results is rather weak, many governments around the world continue to view cultural education as an interesting addition to overall schooling, rather than an integral part of it.

Meanwhile, Bourdieu's notion of the importance of 'high culture' and its connection with a ruling elite has been much challenged, in part by those who argue that cultural tastes have become much more diverse and who cast doubt on the existence of a high-culture ruling elite (Chan and Goldthorpe 2007). What is sometimes known as the 'cultural omnivore' thesis (Peterson and Kern 1996) maintains that the primary distinction between types of cultural consumer is between 'omnivores' – those who consume a wide range of culture, from opera, theatre and museums to popular music, film, TV and videogames – and cultural 'univores', whose tastes are more limited. The implication of this is that 'cultural capital' no longer resides purely in knowing about Beethoven or Molière, still less no doubt in only knowing about TV soap operas, but involves a comfortable acquaintance with both high and popular culture – the ability to switch from knowledge of cutting-edge literary fiction to appreciation of videogames and TV adverts.

However, as Miles and Sullivan argue (2010), the cultural omnivore thesis, though persuasive, should not be taken to mean that the social distinctions between forms of cultural consumption have collapsed. It may be that the distinction between omnivores and univores is still an expression of social inequality – knowledge of popular culture is now widespread, but knowledge of, or participation in some cultural forms remains very limited. Since

2005 the Department of Culture Media and Sport (DCMS) in the UK, together with many of the agencies that it supports, have been researching participation in culture and sport on an annual basis. The outcome, published as *Taking Part*, is a continuous survey which began with a weighted sample of nearly 30,000 adults in England, with material released quarterly.

While headline figures seem positive – almost three-quarters of adults in England have visited a heritage site, half have visited a museum or gallery and almost 80 per cent have participated in some sort of arts event – once these numbers are broken down to particular cultural forms, the number of non-participants becomes evident. Some cultural forms – dance performances of any sort, opera, literary festivals and talks – attract less than 5 per cent of respondents, crafts fairs attract around 10 per cent of the population, while musicals, often seen as the mainstay of commercial theatre, attract around 20 per cent (DCMS 2012; see Chapter 1 for more discussion on cultural participation statistics).

This does not mean that cultural activities are not popular: 90.2 per cent of adults reported watching TV as their main leisure time activity (even more popular than time spent with family and friends), and nearly 80 percent said their main leisure time activity was listening to music (DCMS 2012). However, the data suggest that participation in cultural activities outside the home remains a core activity for only a small minority of people, with a large penumbra of very occasional attendees and around a quarter of the population taking no part at all. In policy terms one might ask: why does this matter? People have different pastimes. They seek to differentiate themselves according to particular cultural tastes and associate themselves with others who share their passions. So what?

As with all areas of public policy and public spending, however, legitimacy is vital and while research suggests that even those who are not frequent arts attendees are generally willing to see public money spent on culture, it remains a relatively easy target for government spending cuts. In addition, if public policy assumes that culture is important then it has to be concerned about grave inequalities in access. More importantly for the topic of this chapter, while the notion that a high-culture elite is simply subsidising its own interests via public spending is difficult to sustain, it is clear that cultural participation remains highly unequal and public policy has done little to successfully combat this.

The alleged 'collapse' of the distinction between popular and high culture is not yet reflected in public policy. Indeed, the creative economy debate referred to above, with its reinstatement of the distinction between commercial and non-commercial cultural activities, threatens to cement the difference further, and while popular culture is celebrated for its economic vitality, its cultural importance remains neglected. Thus, small bookshops and record shops are rarely considered worthy of protecting in planning decisions, nightclubs can close or be turned into apartments, videogames receive none of the public support given to film, and popular sports can be made available only on pay TV. These could all be construed as matters relevant to cultural policy – all involve sites where people are exposed to culture – but policy-makers seem content to leave such issues to often ineffectual competition regulation. As we shall see throughout this book, one of the greatest difficulties that policymakers face is dealing with questions of market power in contemporary cultural production. It is an issue that has concerned many academic commentators on the cultural industries, but as the next section suggests, the links between academia and cultural policymakers have rarely been particularly strong.

THE STUDY OF CULTURAL POLICY

Insofar as it represents a distinct discipline within universities and other research centres, cultural policy studies largely grew out of cultural studies (rather than, say, political science or policy studies), and this in part explains what we have argued is its disconnection from studies of public policy more generally (see Chapter 3). Within cultural studies, a relatively small but prominent group of scholars have argued for the salience of studying cultural policy – Angela McRobbie (1996: 335) called it the 'missing agenda of cultural studies' – though often from different theoretical standpoints.

In his account of cultural policy studies, Stuart Cunningham (2003) sees it as a 'centrist' or 'reformist' response to what he believes to be the limitations of cultural studies:

> the reflex anti-capitalism, anti-consumerism and romanticisation of sub-cultural resistance embodied in the classical texts of cultural studies are no longer adequate responses to the big questions confronting the articulation of politics and culture in modern Western societies.
>
> (Cunningham 2003: 13)

Within cultural policy studies, one of the major debates has been about how culture is defined (the subject of this chapter) and the implications of these definitional debates for policy. One argument, associated with the work of Tony Bennett (1992), is based on an instrumental or 'useful' notion of culture and conceptualised with reference to Foucault's theory of governmentality. The second, articulated most clearly by Jim McGuigan (1996, 2004), is based on a communicative notion of culture, conceptualised with reference to Habermas' notion of the public sphere.

Bennett's argument was that the emancipatory politics espoused by many in cultural studies had little force without real engagement with the institutions and systems of cultural governance. His idea for making cultural studies 'useful' was 'the training of cultural technicians: that is, of intellectual workers less committed to cultural critique as an instrument for changing consciousness, than to modifying the functioning of culture by means of technical adjustments to its governmental deployment' (Bennett 1992: 406). In other words, engagement with the processes of policymaking did not have to be corrupting but could lead to more enlightened cultural policies, particularly at the level of cultural institutions such as the museum or concert hall. In response McGuigan criticised Bennett's approach, particularly for what he saw as its lack of critical distance from power structures. A version of this debate has recently surfaced in connection with writing on the creative industries, with Schlesinger (2009) arguing that many of the academic community researching or teaching in the area have been part of what he terms the 'Hallelujah Chorus' of approval for these notions, rather than acting as critical commentators. Clearly there remains a significant divide in views even among scholars of cultural policy as to what their 'project' should be (different approaches to researching cultural policy are discussed in Chapter 3).

Almost by definition, studies of cultural policy outside of the academy, often commissioned by government or quasi-governmental agencies, are more likely to be in the 'applied' (or in Adorno's terms 'administrative') tradition, though this does not mean that they cannot comment critically on the development of policy. As Scullion and Garcia (2005) argue in their case study of cultural policymaking in Scotland following the first phases of devolution, the types of data and evidence consulted (and even in some cases, the questions asked) may be the same in critical or applied policy research, but the context is generally framed rather differently. Put simply, questions for applied research are more likely to be 'how' than 'why' questions. The example they give is the debate about Scottish nationalism within Scottish cultural policy, a notion which, they argue, has been critically examined within the academy but in terms of cultural policy study is treated as a rather unproblematic concept (see Chapter 5).

Despite debates about the utility and purpose of studying cultural policy, the growth of the creative economy as a global policy discourse has driven an increased interest in cultural policy, both within and outside the academy, and has also increased its breadth. Cultural policy studies are a common component of media and cultural studies courses, and are also growing in other areas of arts education (fine art, theatre studies, fashion and design, museum studies, and so on) as well as in fields such as festival and events management. The range of disciplines with which it may now be associated is an indication that it has moved on from being simply the study of arts policy or public policy for subsidised culture; in addition, as this chapter has argued, it has had to embrace our changing understanding of what constitutes the culture of cultural policy.

CONCLUSIONS

Deciding the remit of cultural policy is one of the most difficult of the challenges facing the cultural policymaker and those who study cultural policy. It has changed over time, moving from a primary concern with the civilising influence of the high arts to a broader concern with a variety of modes of expression and entertainment. It differs by geography; even an international policy idea like the creative industries is understood differently in different countries, sometimes including fashion or advertising, sometimes not; sometimes as broad as food or tourism and sometimes largely focussed on digital technology. And crucially, it is determined by *politics*. While the idea of some public support for culture is a relatively settled policy debate in many European countries, what constitutes 'culture' has differed between administrations (see Chapter 5). In other cases, the difference is less party political and more about broad ideologies: conservatives versus liberals; authoritarians versus libertarians; the religious versus the secular.

All of these issues will have a bearing on what we see as 'culture' and why we might feel that public policy has a role in it, as well as what we think that role should be. Remembering this should alert us to the fact that cultural policy is not simply a question of administration, deciding what gets funded or how to measure the size of the film industry, but something that engages with questions of values, beliefs and priories in a very fundamental way.

NOTES

1 What is generally collectively known as 'Culture and Anarchy' was published by Arnold as a series of articles in *The Cornhill Magazine* between 1867 and 1875.

2 A statutory conservation charity, more generally associated with preserving historic houses and stately homes, as well as green spaces.

REFERENCES AND FURTHER READING

Adorno, T. (1991) *The Culture Industry: Selected Essays on Mass Culture*, London: Routledge.

Adorno, T. and Horkheimer, M. (1944) *The Culture Industry: Enlightenment as Mass Deception*. Available at www.marxists.org/reference/archive/adorno/1944/culture-industry.htm (accessed 23/11/13).

——(1947 *Dialectic of Enlightenment* (as *Dialektik der Aufklärung*), Amsterdam: Querido Verlag; G. S. Noerr (ed.), E. Jephcott (trans.) (2002), Stanford CA: Stanford University Press.

Amin, A. and Thrift, N. (eds) (2004) *Cultural Economy: a Reader*, Blackwell: Oxford.

Andari, R., Bakhshi, H., Hutton, W., O'Keeffe, A. and Schneider, P. (2007) *Staying Ahead: the Economic Performance of the UK's Creative Industries*, London: The Work Foundation.

Bamford, A. (2006) *The Wow Factor: Global Research Compendium on the Impacts of Arts in Education*, New York: Waxman Munster.

Beckett, A. (2010) *When the Lights Went Out. What Really Happened to Britain in the Seventies*, London: Faber and Faber.

Bennett, T. (1992) 'Putting policy into cultural studies', in L. Grosberg, C. Nelson and P. Treichler (eds) *Cultural Studies*, London: Routledge.

——(1998) *Culture: a Reformer's Science*, London: Sage.

Bennett, T., Savage, M., Silva, E., Warde, A., Gayo-Cal, M. and Wright, D. (2009) *Culture, Class, Distinction*, London: Routledge.

Beriss, D. and Sutton, D. (eds) (2007) *The Restaurants Book: Ethnographies of Where we Eat*, London: Berg.

Bevir, M. and Rhodes, R. (2003) Interpreting British Governance, London: Routledge.

Bianchini, F. (1987) 'GLC R I P, 1981–1986', *New Formations*, 1: 103–17.

——(1993) 'Remaking European cities: the role of cultural policies', in F. Bianchini and M. Parkinson (eds) *Cultural Policy and Urban Regeneration: the West European Experience*. Manchester: Manchester University Press.

Bourdieu, P. (1984) *Distinction: a Social Critique of the Judgment of Taste*, Cambridge MA: Harvard University Press.

British Council (2010) *Mapping the Creative industries: a Toolkit*, London: British Council.

Chan, T. and Goldthorpe, J. (2007) 'The social stratification of cultural consumption: some policy implications of a research project', *Cultural Trends*, 16(4): 373–84.

Cowen, T. (1998) *In Praise of Commercial Culture*, Cambridge MA: Harvard University Press.

Cunningham, S. (2003) 'Cultural studies from the viewpoint of cultural policy', in J. Lewis and T. Miller (eds) *Critical Cultural Policy Studies: a Reader*, Oxford: Blackwell.

——(2009) 'Trojan Horse or Rorschach Blot? Creative industries discourse around the world', *International Journal of Cultural Policy*, 15(4): 375–86.

DCMS (2001) *Creative Industries Mapping Document*, London: DCMS.

——(2012) *Taking Part 2012/13 Quarter 1 Statistical Release*, London: DCMS.

Doyle, G. (2013) *Understanding Media Economics*, London: Sage.

Garnham, N. 1987. 'Concepts of culture: public policy and the cultural industries', *Cultural Studies*, 1(1): 23–37.

——(1990) *Capitalism and Communication: Global Culture and the Economics of Information*, London: Sage.

——(2005) 'From cultural to creative industries', *International Journal of Cultural Policy*, 11(1): 15–29.

Gibson, C. (2011) 'Cultural economy: achievements, divergences, future prospects', *Geographical Research*, 50(3): 1–10.

Gray, C. (2010) 'Analysing cultural policy: incorrigibly plural or ontologically incompatible?' *International Journal of Cultural Policy,* 16(2): 215–30.

Hebdige, D. (1979) *Subculture: the Meaning of Style,* London: Routledge.

Hesmondhalgh, D. (2002) *The Cultural Industries,* London: Sage.

——(2005) 'Media and public policy as cultural policy: the case of the British Labour government', *International Journal of Cultural Policy,* 11(1): 95–108.

——(2008) 'Cultural and creative industries' in T. Bennett and J. Frow (eds) *The Sage Handbook of Cultural Analysis,* London: Sage.

——2012. *The Cultural Industries,* third edition, London: Sage.

Higgs, P., Cunningham, S. and Bakhshi, H. (2008) *Beyond the Creative Industries: Mapping the Creative Economy.* London: NESTA.

Hoggart, R. (1957) *The Uses of Literacy,* London: Chatto and Windus.

Jenkins, T. (2012) '"Who are we to decide?" Internal challenges to cultural authority in the contestation over human remains in British museums', *Cultural Sociology* 6(3): 455–70.

Keynes, J. M. (1982) *The Collected Writings of John Maynard Keynes,* vol. 28 (ed. D. Moggridge), London: Macmillan Press.

Lambeth (2010) *Wellbeing through Culture: Developing a Cultural Commissioning Strategy for Lambeth.* Available at www.lambeth.gov.uk/NR/rdonlyres/4F898683-75A0-443A-93AD-8FC2FFA9EF1E/0/ActivateCultivateCreate.pdf (accessed 28/11/13).

Lash, S. and Lury, C. (2007) *Global Culture Industry: the Mediation of Things,* Cambridge: Polity Press.

Lewis, J. and Miller, T. (eds) (2003) *Critical Cultural Policy Studies. a Reader,* Oxford: Blackwell.

Looseley, D. (1995) *The Politics of Fun: Cultural Policy and Debate in Contemporary France,* Oxford: Berg.

MacDonald, I. (2003) *The People's Music,* London: Pimlico.

McGuigan, J. (1996) *Culture and the Public Sphere,* London: Routledge.

——(2004) *Rethinking Cultural Policy,* Maidenhead: Open University Press.

McRobbie, A. (1996) 'All the world's a stage, screen or magazine: when culture is the logic of late capitalism', *Media, Culture and Society,* 18(3): 335–42.

Miege, B. (1989) *The Capitalization of Cultural Production,* New York: International General.

Miles, A. and Sullivan, A. (2010) *Understanding the Relationship between Taste and Value in Culture and Sport,* London: DCMS.

Myerscough, J. (1998) *The Economic Importance of the Arts in Great Britain,* London: Policy Studies Institute.

NESTA (2006) *Creating Growth: How the UK Can Develop World-class Creative Businesses,* London: NESTA.

——(2013) *A Manifesto for the Creative Economy,* London: NESTA.

Newbigin, J. (2010) *The Creative Economy: An Introductory Guide,* London: British Council.

Oakley, K. (2014) 'Good work? Rethinking cultural entrepreneurship', in C. Bilton and S. Cummings (eds) *The Handbook of Management and Creativity.* London: Edward Elgar.

O'Connor, J. (2004) '"A special kind of city knowledge": innovative clusters, tacit knowledge and the "Creative City"', *Media International Australia*, 112: 131–49.

——(2007) *The Cultural and Creative Industries: a Review of the Literature*, London: Creative Partnerships.

——(2010) *The Cultural and Creative Industries: A Literature Review*, second edition, Creativity, Culture and Education series. London: Creativity Culture and Education.

Peterson, R. and Kern, R. (1996) 'Changing highbrow taste: from snob to omnivore', *American Sociological Review*, 61(5): 900–7.

Sandbrook, D. (2012) *Seasons in the Sun: the Battle for Britain 1974–1979*, London: Allen Lane.

Schlesinger, P. (2009) 'Creativity and experts: New Labour, think tanks and the policy process', *The International Journal of Press/Politics*, 14(1): 3–20.

Scullion, A. and Garcia, B. (2005) 'What is cultural policy research?' *International Journal of Cultural Policy*, 11(2): 113–27.

Stiglitiz, J., Sen, A. and Fitoussi, J. (2009) *Report by the Commission on the Measurement of Economic Performance and Social Progress*. Available at www.stiglitz-sen-fitoussi.fr/documents/rapport_anglais.pdf (accessed 01/08/13).

Storey, J. (2006) *Cultural Theory and Popular Culture: an Introduction*, fourth edition, Harlow: Pearson Education.

Throsby, D. (2010) *The Economics of Cultural Policy*, Cambridge: Cambridge University Press.

UNESCO (2013) *The Creative Economy Report: Widening Local Development Pathways*, New York: UNESCO.

Upchurch, A. (2004) 'John Maynard Keynes, the Bloomsbury group and the origins of the Arts Council movement', *International Journal of Cultural Policy*, 10(2): 203–17.

van Heur, B. (2008) *Networks of Aesthetic Production and the Urban Political Economy*, unpublished PhD thesis, University of Freien, Berlin.

Williams, R. (1958) *Culture and Society*, London: Chatto and Windus.

——(1973) 'Base and superstructure in Marxist cultural theory', *New Left Review*, 82; reprinted in R. Williams (1980), *Culture and Materialism: Selected Essays*, London: Verso.

——(1981a) *Culture*, London: Fontana.

——(1981b) 'Politics and policies: the case of the Arts Council', in *The Arts Council: Politics and Policies*, Arts Council of Great Britain; reprinted in R. Williams (1989), *The Politics of Modernism: Against the New Conformists*. London: Verso.

Wollen, P. (2012) *Singin' in the Rain*. London: BFI.

3

THE POLICY OF CULTURAL POLICY

Having worked through contrasting definitions and uses of 'culture' in the last chapter, it is now time to turn our attention to the second keyword of our title – policy – and ask and answer a seemingly simple question: what is cultural *policy*? This question, it turns out, is only seemingly simple: as with Chapter 2, as soon as we embark on the quest for definition, we quickly find ourselves in complex terrain, for what the policy of cultural policy actually is, what policy means when wedded to culture, and a whole raft of related questions soon break the surface, as do questions about who makes cultural policy, at what geographical scales, for what purposes and with what effects (and note here that purpose and effect are not always the same thing).

But let's begin with a simple answer: cultural policy is the branch of public policy concerned with the administration of culture. As ever with the work of definition, we are immediately thrown into a chain of signification: what is public policy? What is policy? What is public? Thankfully, the well-established field of policy studies has been pondering this particular issue for some time and has developed a diverse toolkit to interrogate this very question (see later in the chapter). Kevin Mulcahy (2006: 265) borrows this succinct definition from Thomas Dye (2005): 'public policy is what governments choose to do or not to do'. Public policy is, Mulcahy continues, 'the sum of government activities' – hence cultural policy becomes the sum of government activities in relation to culture, or what governments choose to do or not to do in relation to culture. This statement reminds us that we need to attend to the issues of government and choice as well as to what Mulcahy (2006: 268) calls the 'ecological complexity' of public policy: that cultural policy does not exist in isolation from government activities and choices in a whole host of policy/political domains – economic policy, welfare and social policy, foreign policy and so on. But it is very important to restate the simple point that cultural policy, as we understand and analyse it in this book, is a form of public policy – important because, as Dave Hesmondhalgh (2005: 96) comments, within studies of cultural (and media) policy, 'it sometimes seems to be forgotten ... that these are areas of public policy more generally'. This forgetting has potentially serious consequences for the practice of cultural policy analysis and for the remit of the emerging inter-disciplinary enterprise of 'cultural policy studies'.

Back to definition: as noted above, public policy is what governments do. But what does 'government' mean here? Does it mean national government, the passing of laws, parliamentary debates, the work of ministers and central government ministries? Certainly it does mean this, but not *only* this. Public policy works at a range of geographical scales, from the local to the global, and cultural policy is no different (hence our attention in subsequent chapters to these different scales). As Deborah Stevenson *et al*. (2010: 159) write, 'Cultural policy is now the province of all levels of government as well as supra-state bodies such as the European Union'. As they go on to describe, there is a dense network or cartography of 'policy circuits' across and between these scales – cultural policy's ecological complexity is in part due to this multi-scalar landscape. And, as we show in Chapters 4 to 6, at each scale we uncover particular niches where policies can come into being: cultural policy is not a simple top-down hierarchy whereby central government cascades policy agendas 'down' to regional and local scales (though there are examples of this, as we will see). This also means being attentive to the 'Who?' question, which we address below.

So cultural policy is what governments at various scales choose to do or not to do in relation to culture. But what is it that they are choosing to do (or not to do) when they are choosing to do something in relation to culture? Here we come to a major fork in the road; on one side we have what might be labelled the *regulation* of culture, and on the other what we might call support for or *promotion* of culture. In terms of the former, we can include issues to do with censorship, protection (for example, from market forces), ownership (for example, of the press) and so on. The latter includes patronage, state funding for culture, etc. In practice much cultural policy includes elements of both regulation and promotion, perhaps more so today than ever before. And promotion of culture also means the promotional uses of culture – or what Raymond Williams (1984) called cultural policy as display (and which he distinguished from 'cultural policy proper'; see also McGuigan 2004). Regulation and promotion are intertwined in policies which require, for example, local governments to produce strategies that audit and promote local cultural assets (an example we will return to later in this chapter).

The discussion above has used a somewhat abstract, general term to discuss the actor(s) involved in cultural policy-making: *government*. Even with the added nuance of geographical scale, we are nevertheless corralling together a diverse body of real actors under the umbrella of government. So, at this juncture, we need to get specific: who actually makes policy and what does the act of policymaking entail?

CULTURAL POLICYMAKERS

Within the broader sphere of policy analysis, there has been considerable debate about this 'Who?' question. Questions have been raised about power and influence, about networks and connections, about forms of action and capacities to act, about the interplay between individuals, institutions and environments, about beliefs and ideas. We also have to wrestle with that age-old conundrum of the balance between structure and agency. What this means, according to Paul Cairney (2012: 4), is that 'public policy is difficult to study [and that] the policy process is complex, messy and often appears to be unpredictable'. But, he rather sweetly adds, 'it is worth the effort'. Once we begin to unravel the 'Who?' question, we move into this messy world of actors acting (or not) within specific contexts, with particular outcomes in mind, and whose actions produce effects (some intended, some not). We are also dealing with issues of organisational structure and culture and with issues to do with policymaking as *work*, as a profession. And, of course, we are dealing with *politics*: with decision-making set in the context of both capital-P Politics and with other forms of politics, such as interdepartmental (and interpersonal) rivalries, attempts to claim a particular agenda or issue, attempts to gain favour, contests over priorities and resources.

Cairney (2012) draws out some of these ways of acting, professionally and politically, and discusses the role of case studies and 'thick description' in research that seeks to narrate the policy process. Among the approaches he outlines is the policy cycle approach, which consists of five stages in the lifecycle of a policy: agenda setting, policy formulation, legitimation, implementation, evaluation, and policy maintenance, succession or termination. While rightly sceptical of such tidy models, Cairney shows that one merit of this approach is that it breaks up policymaking into component parts, and this allows us to consider the role of different actors at different moments. At particular stages in the cycle we can identify the role played by numerous actors, including government ministers and other elected political actors, civil servants, bureaucrats and technocrats, quangos, think tanks, lobbyists, consultants, academics (sometimes acting as consultants), 'street-level bureaucrats' who are often charged with actually delivering policy on the ground (a museum curator might be a suitably cultural example), and the public (often roped into the policy process through forms of consultation). Again, we need also to consider geographical scale here, as well as the relative balance of 'top-down' and 'bottom-up' approaches (not all policies emanate from the mind of the government's culture minister, if the government even has one). And we might need to at least acknowledge a very significant actor in the cultural sphere whose influence shapes cultural policy in myriad ways: the market (Pratt 2005). Combining the breaking up of the policy cycle with this roll call of actors and the emphasis on case studies steers us inevitably towards providing some thick description of our own, through a case study to which we now turn.

WHO MADE LOCAL CULTURAL STRATEGIES?

Our case study comes from personal experience of involvement in a particular cycle of cultural policymaking in the UK. While it might seem like a simple 'top-down' story of central government agenda setting followed by local-level implementation, the tale unfolds in a more complicated fashion, moving across and between policy domains, shuttling from actor to actor. The background to this particular moment in UK cultural policymaking is more comprehensively covered by others (e.g. Gilmore 2004; Gray 2004), but simply laid out it 'begins' with the issuing of a document by the UK central government's Department of Culture, Media and Sport (DCMS) in 1999. This document, *Local Cultural Strategies* (DCMS 1999a), outlined a new, joined-up approach to cultural planning, which required all local authorities in England to produce a cultural policy and action plan. Two other related documents should be flagged up here: *Regional Cultural Consortiums* (DCMS 1999b) which added to the joining-up agenda by connecting local authority cultural planning at the regional scale, and *Creating Opportunities* (DCMS 2000), which contained revised guidance on local-level policies. For the cultural sector, this agenda represented something of a high-water mark, requiring local authorities to audit, celebrate, plan for and deliver continuing cultural opportunities, across the country. Many finished strategies were launched with considerable fanfare (though not all, as we shall see). Culture was suddenly highly visible, as well as being tasked with addressing many non-cultural agendas (Gray 2004). The flurry of activity also led to countless opportunities for consultants to offer their services to assist local authorities in the strategy making process – and that is where we come in.

At this moment, something was also happening in higher education institutions: academics were being encouraged to

consider engagement outside the campus and think more entrepreneurially about the marketable expertise they could tout in the
name of knowledge transfer and income diversification (Selwood
2006). David happened to be working in a cultural studies
department at the time, in a humanities and social sciences faculty
that was struggling to enter this new marketplace. Together with
colleagues, he established a consultancy, CTU, to engage with
cultural policymaking in the particular locality he was working
in. CTU undertook creative industries mapping work and various
other projects to do with culture, and offered its services to local
authorities now attempting to develop cultural strategies (as well
as working on a county-wide scale). Successfully parlaying a rather
academic skillset and the credentials of a university, CTU was soon
contracted to assist local authority officers with consultation and
policy formulation (for a fuller account see Bell 2007).

The first thing to remark on is that each of the half-dozen local
authorities in the county had a different set-up in terms of who was
responsible for heading-up the local cultural strategy work. CTU
worked with arts development officers, sport, leisure and recreation
officers, economic development officers, and indirectly with elected
councillors responsible for 'culture' portfolios (often alongside
other things). So, in terms of *dramatis personae*, we already have
central government ministers (and accompanying civil servants,
who no doubt actually produced the DCMS documents), local
authority elected members and (unelected) officers of various
stripes, and academics/consultants. In each different job they
undertook, the balance of responsibility was different, the extent
of their input was different, the extra cast members drawn in
were different, and the outcome was different.

To give just one example: one local authority that engaged the
services of CTU was a relatively affluent place well endowed with
'high culture' assets but concerned (for mainly Political reasons)
with the issue of 'hard-to-reach' and 'excluded' groups not well served
by its current cultural offer. The CTU team spent a particularly
memorable evening at a local skateboard park, attempting to engage
young people who mainly came from less well-off peripheral
neighbourhoods and who felt doubly marginalised by the poor
facilities they were provided with and by their lack of interest in

much of what the council was billing as its cultural riches. In due course CTU distilled these findings into a finished document, which the local council officer was pleased to take off our hands and progress as the local cultural strategy. But local elections were looming, and suddenly a strategy which shone a light on the council's failings as much as it trumpeted its successes became somewhat unpalatable. Where once prioritising the needs of 'hard-to-reach' groups seemed a perfect way to show aliveness to current cultural (and social, economic, health, etc.) agendas, now it seemed a bit risky. The strategy quietly disappeared from view. There was no fanfare and no launch. The skateboarders were not invited to endorse the council's new, inclusive strategy. As soon as the elected councillor saw the consultation materials – materials that the council had specifically asked to be included in the document – the document was pulled. As it happened, events soon took over, as local cultural strategies became de-prioritised by central government, folded instead into 'community strategies' (DCMS 2004; Gray 2004).

We have told this tale in order to address the 'Who?' question: in this case study, who were the key policymakers? Was it the DCMS, which issued the initial edict requiring everyone to produce a local cultural strategy? Clearly this was an important catalyst, and without it we would not have witnessed the brief cultural gold rush. But beyond having the initial idea and laying out some guidelines, the DMCS passed on responsibility ... to the local level. On the ground, then, various players joined in: local authority elected councillors seized the moment to push their portfolio closer to the centre; local authority officers, often poorly resourced and dealing with even more complex portfolios, also seized the moment, for various motives (some altruistic, some less so). But, because of their meagre resources and overstretched personnel, a lot of local authorities outsourced the work of actually producing the strategy to assorted consultants, freelancers and 'para-academics'. These actors too were motivated by particular concerns (in our case, income diversification as a form of job security, but also a broader desire to be *useful*; on the pros and cons of this, see Bell 2007). As part of their role, members of CTU facilitated workshops with representatives from each local authority that chose to use our services and carried out various forms of consultation (not just with skateboarders, though they are a particularly interesting case). CTU used the words of those they consulted to shape the document that, in the story recounted above, was handed to the council officer, who handed it to the portfolio-holding elected member of the council. Who shelved it, before central government itself had a change of heart and subsumed all local cultural strategies within the new top priority, 'community strategies' (Gilmore 2004; Gray 2004).

Who, then, made (or unmade) this cultural strategy? Clearly, everyone played a part. If the strategy had lived on, as others CTU contributed to did, then we'd also have to add in those 'street-level bureaucrats' tasked with actually making things happen, as well as the people given the job of evaluation, monitoring, revision (to complete the first run of the policy cycle). This quick burst of thick description, then, teases out some of the complexity behind the issue of who makes cultural policy. While each case (study) will be different, we can nevertheless pick out some general lessons here, in terms of needing to understand the 'ecological complexity' of policymaking and policymakers. In some quarters this has led to a more ethnographic or 'anthropological' approach to studying the policy process (Shore and Wright 1997; Stevens 2011), not to mention a series of 'confessional' tales from other players caught up in the business of actually making policy (Selwood 2006; Worpole 1998). But we must not lose sight of other forces at work here; Hesmondhalgh (2005: 106) warns against overemphasising the agency of policymakers at the expense of considering external constraints and 'the wider forces at work behind policy' – in his case, the issue of globalisation is highlighted as an important constraint shaping media and cultural policy in the UK under New Labour's administration (cf. the Australian case, explored by Craik *et al.* 2003).

As already noted, the policy analysis literature has considered (and reconsidered) issues of structure and agency in its accounting for the forces shaping policymaking, as well as developing its own conceptual vocabulary to give its discussions clarity (Cairney 2012). One outcome is, perhaps inevitably, a more *complicated* account of policymaking, as well as divergent theories and methods brought into play. As we'll see later in the chapter, when it comes to cultural policy analysis, similar trends are evident. But at this moment we would want to half agree, half disagree with Hesmondhalgh: it is important to understand the many different actors that contribute, in different ways, to policymaking, while not forgetting the impact of various external, structural forces. It is only by bringing the two perspectives together, ultimately, that we can begin to fathom the policy process. And, we would argue, this kind of storytelling is important because policies too often seem to appear by magic, with no context or backstory; cultural policy can be a 'black box' whose inner workings are hard to discern (Nisbett 2013b).

External forces take many forms, too: from multifaceted processes such as globalisation or economic restructuring, to geopolitical pressures of various sorts, to the 'memetic' spread of ideas that diffuse across geographical and policy landscapes. In the case described above, economic forces are certainly at work in pushing policymakers to consider the uses of culture to address numerous problems and issues; so too is the diffusion of this very idea, that culture can be put to many uses. Later, when we discuss policy attachment and policy mobility, we'll flesh out this argument in more depth. For now it's sufficient to flag up that external forces were certainly at work in shaping the agenda that led, ultimately, to the DCMS documents outlining how local authorities should view culture *strategically*. For now, though, we want to move from 'Who?' to 'What?'.

CULTURAL POLICY AS OBJECT

Earlier we somewhat skated over the definition of cultural policy; despite arguing that it's the part of public policy concerned with culture, already defined, we left cultural policy as a rather abstract concept. In the local cultural strategy case outlined above, we get some indication of what this particular policy is (or was): an actual, material document, with words and pictures (Gilmore 2004). Here we want to consider other cases, to get a sense of the form, status, and 'thingness' of cultural policy. This will lead us to also consider the question of *effects*: how does cultural policy work? What does it do? And how are these effects embedded in its form? After that we can consider the implications of all this for how we study, research and analyse cultural policy.

So, if we want to hold a cultural policy in our hands, to touch and feel it, where can we go? (Let's set aside for now the growing digitisation of public policy, and hence its dematerialisation.) Well, to return to local cultural strategies for a moment, in one of the other places CTU worked, a final material document was produced – or, rather, two documents were produced, one a full strategy designed for internal use in the council and its cultural facilities, the other a shorter public summary, designed and illustrated, which boiled down the main document to soundbites and images. As Abigail Gilmore (2004) showed, there were a number of recurrent motifs in local cultural strategies, which ended up producing something less than the local cultural distinctiveness that the strategies were supposed to highlight. Nevertheless, across the land, many actual physical documents did get made and handed out. But is such a document a simple material reflection of the policy process and distillation of the larger documents that inevitably underpinned local cultural strategy development? Well, yes and no. Public summary documents have different agendas and audiences. They are at least in part promotional. The actual local cultural strategies, complete with action plans and other auditing tools, often spoke a more technical language and addressed an insider readership of professionals in the cultural (and local government) sector. So, perhaps understandably, form and audience intersect through the mode of address.

As we've just alluded to, this particular moment in cultural policymaking bears clear traces of a broader shift in the technologies of cultural governance, symbolised by things like audits and the trend towards evidence-based policy (in the discussion above, the consultation with the skateboarders was partly fulfilling this requirement). As Eleanore Belfiore (2004: 183) recounts, such moves are symptoms of a bigger ideological shift that produced what has come to be called the 'new public management' (NPM) – a different approach to public policy, a new 'style of public administration' that places emphasis on measurement, data collection, evaluation, target setting, value for money, performance indicators, and a whole host of new metrics for assessing 'success'. This change is reflected in the form, content, address and style of cultural policy documents, which in many cases have become classic examples of 'NPMisation'. We'll return to the question of why the public (subsidised) cultural sector might have become a key site to witness NPM at work when we turn our attention to the debate about the 'instrumentalisation' of culture. For now, the important thing to stress is that cultural policies take on particular forms as a result of both endogenous and exogenous forces. When we hold a policy document in our hands and try to get a reading from it, we need to be mindful of the conditions of its production.

We've begun this discussion in a seemingly simple place: local cultural strategies are an unambiguous example of cultural policy – if we can sidestep the definitional and operational distinction between policy and strategy – and one we can (at least sometimes) hold in our hands. Other policies might be harder to find, harder to handle. In this regard, we're taken back to the issue of definition: when is a public policy classifiable as a *cultural* policy? Jeremy Ahearne (2009) makes a useful (though not unproblematic) distinction here between what he labels 'explicit' and 'implicit' cultural policy. Local cultural strategies exemplify the former, being explicitly about culture. The latter category Ahearne defines like this:

> Within the domain of 'implicit' cultural policies, one might ... distinguish between the unintended cultural side effects of various kinds of policy and those deliberate courses of action intended to shape cultures but which are not expressly thematised as such.
>
> (Ahearne 2009: 144)

For Ahearne, then, it might be harder to know if what you're holding in your hand is a cultural policy, especially when it lacks the express thematisation that can be a giveaway. As he adds, this means that 'the most important forms of cultural policy [are] not always where people [think] they are' (ibid.). This is quite a conundrum; where are we to 'draw the line' in terms of policies that we would include as part of our analysis and those that are outside our concern? As different studies have variously shown,

social and welfare policy, economic policy and foreign policy –
among other policy domains – can contain implicit cultural policies
(Nisbett 2013b). Clive Gray (2004) has developed the idea of
'policy attachment' to explain how, in this case, culture can
'attach' itself to other areas of public policy. Echoing Ahearne,
this means that cultural policy does not always exist in its own silo,
is not always the purview of those whose job titles contain the
word 'culture', and moreover any outcome anticipated from
the implementation of the policy might not directly impact on
culture (though it might, in both anticipated and unanticipated
ways). Sometimes we have to look quite hard at a policy to decide
whether it's part of our purview, too.

The notion of implicitness might take us in other investigative
directions, too. For example, we might ask: when is a policy not a
policy? What features does a policy have to have in order to be
classified as such? This is perhaps especially pertinent (and complicated), in situations, like that in the UK, where a great deal of
cultural policy is governed by the so-called 'arm's-length' principle –
where direct government involvement in culture is limited to
granting various intermediary organisations (sometimes labelled
quangos), certain decision-making powers and devolving budgets
for them to allocate – the Arts Council being the best-known
example (on its history, see Hewison 1995; see also Chapter 5).

Other national governments take much more directive control of
cultural policy, variously described as 'architects' (the example of
France is often given here) or 'engineers' (China exemplifies this
variant) (Gray 2008). Can we say that, in the UK, arm's length
is *the* cultural policy of the nation-state, as we might say that US
cultural policy is limited to tax incentive schemes and so is even
more hands-off? This would be a very narrow definition of cultural
policy indeed; instead, we must expand our horizons to consider
the various bodies that administer the public cultural sector –
bodies such as the Arts Council. At times, the British government
has even directly intervened in cultural policy, for example through
the passing of acts of parliament. Robert Hewison (1995) cites a
number of such occasions, beginning with the 1753 act which led
to the creation of the British Museum, and including the formation
of the BBC in 1927 and of the Arts Council of Great Britain in

1946. Here, enshrined in the statutes, we see again unambiguous, explicit cultural policies. At other times, individual cultural institutions (or collaborations between them) might take the driving seat in cultural policymaking – Melissa Nebitt (2013a) provides a case study of the World Collections Programme instigated by a cartel of major UK institutions, including the British Library and the Victoria and Albert Museum. Here, via the arm's-length principle, bodies jointly produced a strategy for cultural diplomacy that, while endorsed by parliament, was driven by the institutions themselves. This discussion raises (at least two) further issues. The first concerns the 'tangibility' or 'thingness' of cultural policy: we're interested in policy documents not just as documents but also for their *effects*. In the discussion above, we see concrete effects in terms of the building of a museum or a collection, the staging of exhibitions and events. Cultural policy studies is not limited to policies we can hold in our hands, therefore – we can also visit, enjoy, look at, think with, eat, drink and shop in the outcomes of cultural policies. When we turn to discuss research methods later in the chapter, we will revisit the implications of this breadth in the object of our study.

Second, our earlier discussion of who makes cultural policy needs some additions, in terms of public bodies and their representatives who are granted, thanks to the arm's length principle, with policymaking powers. In his discussion of the 'overlapping zones' of cultural policymakers, Geir Vestheim (2012) highlights four key groups at work: politicians, civil servants, professionals working in cultural institutions, and professional artists. In his Bourdieuvian discussion, these actors occupy different 'fields' that intersect around cultural policy but bring with them different imperatives and perspectives and play out power struggles in the overlapping zone where culture meets politics. Vestheim's insights mean that our view of the ecology of cultural policy is necessarily gaining in complexity, which therefore poses a challenge for the practices of researching policymaking: the need to redraw the boundaries around what is the proper object of our study. In Nisbett's study, one important consequence of her focus on the World Collections Programme and the revelation of its backstory in terms of its genesis from within the cultural institutions is that it enables her to tackle one of the thorniest issues in cultural policy studies – the issue of instrumentalism. In the conventional terms of this debate, cultural policy has progressively been emptied of its important 'art for art's sake' logic, which has been replaced by various (and increasingly numerous) *uses* of culture (Caust 2003).

GOVERNMENT AND THE USES OF CULTURE

Instrumentalism will be a recurring theme in this book, given the prominence of the concept in cultural policy studies (for now we need to set aside the instrumentalism of cultural policy studies itself). Like Gray's (2004) notion of policy attachment, what we are discussing here is a changing emphasis on what culture is for (and therefore what cultural policy is for). This is an age-old debate that overshadows the whole policy domain, asking about the 'correct' (or perhaps 'best') form of cultural policymaking. It asks questions about cultural production and cultural consumption, and about the priorities that follow from this: is it 'better' to fund art classes or art galleries? What kinds of 'good' can culture be asked to do? Royseng (2008) refers to this as cultural policy's 'ritual logic' – the assumption that culture can magically make things (and people) 'better', or make 'better' people (and things). From Gray's perspective, this leads to the 'attaching' of culture to other policy priorities, and in doing so losing sight of the 'intrinsic' value of culture. In short, culture is required to help fix problems identified as priority areas for state action. So the cultural sector might be asked to assist in schemes tackling anti-social behaviour, or social exclusion, or obesity, or poverty. Within cultural policy studies, instrumentalism has tended to be viewed as some sort of top-down imposition that coerces the cultural sector into taking on big problems. But Nisbett (2013a; 2013b) challenges this view – and she is not alone – by exploring how cultural institutions choose to attach themselves to 'non-cultural' domains, in her case foreign policy. Her empirical material reveals a more savvy handling of instrumentalism. As she summarises:

> Instrumentalism is not rejected by those within the cultural institu-
> tions. Funding streams are expected to echo political objectives. This

principle is both adhered to and propagated by the cultural sector itself. All policies are expected to achieve *something* or relate to *something*, and policy inherently involves Government; otherwise there would be no policy.

(Nisbett 2013a: 10, emphasis in original)

While it might be possible to argue cynically that these cultural sector representatives have simply internalised the logics of NPM and neoliberalism more broadly (McGuigan 2005) or are strategically echoing them back in order to gain competitive advantage, Nisbett concludes with a call to rethink instrumentalism, credit the cultural sector with power and agency in the policy process, and track how instrumentalism is used not only in a 'top-down' way to reframe cultural policy but also by the cultural sector itself. After all, as many commentators have agreed, policy is by definition instrumental, in that its aim is to achieve change. Expecting cultural policy to be somehow different seems a misunderstanding of how public policy works – and, again, is a reflection of the forgetting that Hesmondhalgh (2005) noted: cultural policy is public policy, after all, and it is in this sense an 'ordinary' rather than an 'exceptional' domain of policymaking (Vestheim 2012). At the same time, it is important to register the potency of the instrumentalism debate within cultural policy studies and to work to understand why there is such distaste for what is seen as some sort of sell-out of culture by government (Wallinger and Warnock 2000). Even culture ministers have been known to wade into this debate, making arguments both for and against instrumental uses of culture (Smith 1998; Jowell 2004).

One thing that the instrumentalism debate brings to our attention is another set of 'fields' that intersect in an overlapping zone: the professional academic fields of the various researchers and analysts drawn to cultural policymaking as an object of study. There are remarkably different traditions, drawing on different disciplinary heritages and different conceptual, methodological and ideological positions, swirling around the cultural policy studies domain. And so we turn to a 'How?' question: how can we analyse cultural policy? What methods are used by cultural policy researchers?

DOING CULTURAL POLICY STUDIES

> Cultural policy research exists in many contexts, asks many different kinds of question and adopts a wide repertoire of research methodologies from a raft of academic discourses.
>
> (Scullion and Garcia 2005: 113)

This issue – the question of what it is we're doing when we're doing cultural policy research – has been growing in prominence, perhaps as a result of the continuing growth of this particular field of study. Commentary ranges from the celebratory to the anxious, from calls to embrace methodological promiscuity to those that see only irreconcilability and dissonance. There are a number of different routes through this maze: here we want to consider two – a focus on how different disciplinary traditions shape the approaches taken to cultural policy analysis, followed by a discussion of selected examples which typify different methods in practice.

It is more or less taken for granted that cultural policy studies is an interdisciplinary project, and as such is blessed with the strengths and weakness that interdisciplinarity always seems to bring: unencumbered by its own 'canon', it is free to experiment and cherry-pick, but in lacking its own 'canon' it also lacks common ground, a sense of common purpose. In some ways this is symptomatic of any field of policy studies – social or welfare policy research seems no different – in that studying policy always has an element of 'applied-ness' to it, though it is also more than simple application of pre-existing theories and methods to 'real world' cases. Policy researchers in general are caught between critical and applied approaches, perhaps today more than ever, when 'applied-ness' turns into usefulness or relevance or impact and becomes an imperative in order to justify the continued existence of humanities and social science subjects in higher education and academic research. This issue hangs over cultural policy studies, characterised by Scullion and Garcia (2005: 117) as a schism between the 'arts-humanities approach' and the 'applied research tradition' – though they ultimately suggest a possible 'third way', or at least an 'uneasy peace' (125), which means that cultural policy research can be critical *and* applied. Such an uneasy peace is also called for by Oliver Bennett (2004) in his widely cited discussion of the 'torn halves' of cultural policy studies, which begins as a review of two key but very different publications, Mark Schuster's (2002) *Informing Cultural Policy* and Justin Lewis and Toby Miller's co-edited (2003) *Critical Cultural Policy Studies* reader. Bennett sees these two texts as characterising the rift in the field, typified by the different stances in their titles: informing (being practical or relevant) versus being critical. Ultimately, Bennett also acknowledges that a heterogeneous field like ours will inevitably contain different approaches and view-points, different theories and methods – and he urges something like an anti-canonical stand that doesn't try to mend the tear and reunify the halves but rather sees vitality in the 'clash of ideas' (Bennett 2004: 246).

Both more scathing (at least at times) and more comprehensive in its diagnosis of the malaise in cultural policy research is Clive Gray's (2010) intervention, which characterises a field of 'mutual incom-prehension' as a result of disciplinary plurality. He lays out his stall unflinchingly, outlining the reasons he sees for this incomprehension between different approaches rooted in different disciplines:

> The lack of understanding that is displayed derives in the main from: a failure to comprehend the differences between methodologies of analysis that are employed within and between different disciplines; a failure to engage with the broader literature arising from different disciplines; and the existence of stereotypical images concerning dif-ferent disciplines, ontologies, epistemologies and methodologies that are often, at best, misleading and, at worse, simply wrong.
>
> (Gray 2010: 215)

What's useful about Gray's discussion is that he moves from general critique to a deeper level of analysis, drawing out how some of the different disciplines currently contributing to cultural policy studies have brought with them disciplinary baggage that needs handling rather than ignoring. For example, he spots a three-way split in broad methodological approaches between (i) a largely positivist approach favoured by researchers coming to cultural policy studies from an economics background, (ii) the interpretivist work of cultural studies scholars, and (iii) realist methodology used in sociology and political science. Such divergence inflects the very definition of culture that forms the starting point for policy analysis, and then shapes every part of the analytical process – even down to where the final outcomes are published, and therefore who reads them. One thing this means for Gray is that research needs to state much more clearly and categorically what methods have been used and why – as he writes, 'an awareness of the *precise methodologies* that are employed in the study of cultural policies is required to provide a basis for understanding what in particular has been uncovered by different analysts employing different tools' (Gray 2010: 225, our emphasis). To be clear, this is not a call for any kind of methodological orthodoxy; it is, rather, a call for researchers to open up their toolkits for others to see and maybe share. A similar point is made by Melissa Nisbett (2013b: 87), who notes that too often, research which analyses cultural policy documents 'omits empirical and methodological detail' (she also notes that the research that goes into policy documents is also often undisclosed – something we will return to later). This is not to say that cultural policy researchers never play show and tell; it's more that methodological discussion can be backgrounded, relegated to a footnote, or excluded altogether. And sometimes it is frustratingly difficult to divine exactly what has been done in terms of analysis.

Rather than repeat Gray's disciplinary typology of methodological approaches – though we will nod to it when appropriate, for it is a useful guide to unpacking the baggage – here we want to further the discussion by looking at a handful of examples of studies which take different perspectives on what cultural policy is and therefore how to analyse it. We have therefore divided research into four categories: studies of cultural policy as discourse, as text, as process and as practice. As we'll see, this isn't always a tidy categorisation; nevertheless, by uncovering, ontologically and epistemologically, how different analysts have figured the very object of their analysis, we can fathom something about the research design, sources and methods chosen: the link between our understanding of what it is we're studying with the way we thereby go about studying it.

CULTURAL POLICY AS DISCOURSE

Within what Gray labels the interpretivist approaches allied to cultural studies, explorations of cultural policy as a discursive formation are central. In this sense, a discourse is a broad and shared framework for understanding, the product of particular forms of knowledge, which is then embedded in and permeates through society and social and cultural formations and practices. In approaching cultural policy as a discourse, we are asking: what is culture understood to be for, how is it organised so as to produce particular effects, who propagates this understanding and through what means? These questions run deep in cultural policy research, given that policy is a technique of government, aimed at producing particular outcomes – or particular people (Miller and Yudice 2002). Tony Bennett has explored this question in much of his work, attempting to uncover how culture has come to be a form of government and how ideas about the uses and values of culture in this regard have come to coalesce into what we now label cultural policy. In his historical work on the coming-into-being of culture as a tool or form of government, Bennett has explored, among other things, 'the discursive conditions which made it intelligible to nineteenth century cultural reformers that the provision of public libraries, museums, and the like might be of service in making the workingman sober and sexually prudent' (Bennett 1998: 11). How, in other words, did a particular idea about the utility of culture as a way of civilising people – especially working-class people – come into being and 'take hold'? (We should also interrogate the discourse of the uncivilised nature of the working class here, too.) Given that this is a historical project of *recovering*, as he puts it, his toolkit is the (cultural) historian's: documents, archives, published and preserved materials. In his discussion of 'The multiplication of culture's utilities' (1998), he tracks the discourse of the civilising effect of culture through parliamentary and committee reports, nineteenth-century writings, the records and papers of cultural institutions, and so on. Through close reading of the ways in which key actors articulated this discourse, Bennett is able to follow it, charting its consolidation and its transformation – part of this historical approach means being mindful of other currents that altered the course of the idea of culture's civilising effect, such as the impact of Charles Darwin's theory of evolution on understandings of class, conduct and civilisation and on the form and purpose of the museum itself.

An example of a 'contemporary history' of another prominent cultural policy discourse – that of the popular – is provided by David Looseley (2011), who is interested in comparing understandings of popular culture in relation to cultural policy in two contrasting national contexts, the UK and France. Tracking debates about and policies around popular culture since 1945, Looseley begins by observing that 'cultural policy is always polysemic' (367) – its meaning is multiple. In charting how a discourse about the value of popular culture acted as a driver for policy formulation, he picks out some major faultlines, such as shifting priorities over the ideas of excellence versus those of access in determining the project of cultural policy in the UK and France. To plot a route through this, he draws, like Bennett, on published sources and policy documents, though he doesn't have to delve quite as deeply into the archive. He also has a wider variety of media sources to draw from, including radio broadcasts and newspaper articles, not to mention his own personal communication with at least one key player. Equally interesting in this example is Looseley's own disciplinary and national location: he writes as a British specialist in French cultural policy, lately asked to write a history of UK cultural policy for a French-language publication, sponsored by the French Ministry of Culture (Poirrier 2011). As he describes the situation:

> having to write a history of British arts policy in French for speakers of French meant approaching that history with a kind of double vision: as an insider, being British myself with my own lived experience of the arts and political life in the UK, but also as an outsider – at least in so far as I am able to abstract myself from that lived experience by viewing it through a French prism.
>
> (Looseley 2011: 365).

This is an interesting confession, worth a moment's thought: here Looseley implicates himself not only as a scholar of cultural policy but also as a citizen who has been subject to it. He reminds us that cultural policy research is undertaken by particular people, whose own histories and locations (geographical, disciplinary, institutional) interweave with the discourses they seek to explore. While he doesn't explicitly spell out his own stance on popular culture, he nonetheless pushes us to consider how biography matters in cultural policy research – he reminds us that discourses interact with, and shape, real lives, including the lives of researchers.

CULTURAL POLICY AS TEXT

There are various ways of approaching cultural policy as text and we need to tease out some of the differences within this category. First, there are approaches which use tools of linguistic or literary analysis in order to get at the meaning(s) contained in a particular policy-text. This kind of textual analysis itself uses tools as varied as critical discourse analysis (linking text back to discourse, looking at how a discourse becomes articulated in textual form), semiotics and deconstruction (looking for hidden meanings), and is a mainstay of the more textual end of cultural studies, hence sitting mainly within the interpretivist school as defined by Gray (there are, it must be noted, more positivist textual approaches, such as content analysis, which can involve quantifying how often particular words, phrases or ideas appear in a given text). Two examples of different textual approaches can usefully illustrate this range. First, Toby Miller and George Yudice (2002) approach a number of texts, *as texts*, in their broad-ranging discussion of cultural policy. Among them is a document produced by the USA National Endowment for the Arts (NEA), *American Canvas* (Larson 1997). Their reading of this document includes some loose content analysis – they note that its 'two hundred pages have almost nothing to say about art practices or meanings' (65) – and their analysis is focussed throughout on what *American Canvas* says (the language of partnership, uses of the arts in projects such as urban regeneration) and doesn't say. This discussion is located in the context of the NEA's history and the broader story of US cultural policy, and *American Canvas* is therefore read as a manifestation of what Miller and Yudice label 'the new governmentalization' (66) of culture, connecting text to discourse.

Second, as part of her 'strategic review' of local cultural strategies in England, Abigail Gilmore (2004) looked at recurrent definitions of culture (most commonly variants on the Williamsian 'way-of-life' definition) that appear time and again in these policies, as well as picking out different approaches taken within specific local cultural strategy documents to tackle the scope of the strategies as delineated by the DCMS. But Gilmore does not only subject local cultural strategies to a textual analysis. She also considers the strategies as documents, as material objects, and tells the stories of their conception, production and dissemination – hence, she additionally considers the policy process. In terms of thinking about policies as documents, she returns our focus to the 'thingness', the actual material form of policies, particularly through her discussion of the production of 'public-facing' versions that assume and address a public audience rather than only speaking to the policy community. The production of public documents is seen as an act of *translation* – turning an otherwise inward-looking, often quite technical document into something more promotional, even aspirational. One example she gives is *Celebrating Essex*, a county-wide public summary document launched at a splashy conference and handed out on CD-ROM. As she writes, the content, form and impact of local cultural strategies were shaped by many factors, including how they were presented and disseminated to the public. Unfortunately, she was unable to round out her analysis by shifting focus from production to consumption and finding out how audiences actually read the strategies (if at all). This is an important part of the text/document approach, though often rendered difficult either by historical distance – Tony Bennett (1998: 12) notes that this is an 'obvious limitation' of his historical work – or by the practicalities of research. However, in some cases, reception/audience studies are possible, giving an added dimension to the analysis – just as audience and reception studies have come to be an important component of cultural policy itself.

We want to turn briefly to a discussion of policies as 'living documents' which, while it addresses welfare/social policy rather than cultural policy per se, seems to us to offer additional fruitful ways to think about what policy documents are and, crucially, what they do. Shona Hunter (2008) discusses the development of a particular equality and diversity policy, and what especially interests us is her attempt to explore 'the process of doing policy documents' and their psychosocial and affective dimensions. As she puts it, 'documents move us, we move them, they constitute points for collective investment and they connect us to others' (Hunter 2008: 508). Through ethnographic accounting of her own involvement in the policy process, set in the context of audit culture and 'new public management', Hunter sees the document as a 'boundary object' (drawing on actor-network theory among other things) and as an example of organisation in action – documents are living, have a life of their own beyond the act of writing, they are never 'fixed' but are instead 'relational'. How documents 'work' (or not) – the report remains unpublished – is the product of many relatings, comings-together and fallings-apart. As our earlier discussion of involvement with local cultural strategies illustrated, the complex and mundane realities of *doing* policies rarely leads to closure and often produces unintended outcomes. Critics of public policy analysis have suggested that this messy reality is somewhat tidied up in many accounts, including those that present policymaking as a process (Cairney 2012) – but we want to reconsider a process approach rather than simply jettisoning it.

CULTURAL POLICY AS PROCESS

We begin this discussion by sticking with local cultural strategies, and with Gilmore's (2004) 'strategic review', as this provides another good example to work with. She defines key stages in the policy process here as: the production of guidance (in this case from DCMS), forming a team and defining responsibility, establishing the scope and timeline for development, gathering and/or commissioning contextual research and data, holding consultation and discussion events, identifying champions and stakeholders, deciding on how to organise the strategy document, producing, and then disseminating and embedding the finished strategy and its associated infrastructure of action plans and updates, public summaries and launch events. In this version of the tale of local cultural strategies, a fairly clear process is outlined (it began, as noted in our earlier discussion, with DCMS deciding to require local authorities to work up strategies – itself part of a much bigger story about modernising and joining up government agendas, 'new public management', and so on). Of course, as we have already seen, the *actual* process was far from tidy and it is possible to tell an altogether different story, of interdepartmental infighting, missed opportunities, disengagement and deprioritising, and a distinct lack of real joined-up-ness (Gray 2004).

One way to get behind the process focus is to talk to the people making the policy, to hear their accounts of what actually went on, rather than just reading this off from the documents – to take what some label a 'sociological' approach (Magor and Schlesinger 2009). Melissa Nisbett (2013a) makes very productive use of interviews in her discussion of one particular policy's development – the World Collections Programme (WCP). By listening to what various key players say about their involvement with this programme, Nisbett is able to give a different account of who did what and why, and this helps her build an argument that reframes instrumentalism in cultural policy by showing how these players knowingly adopted or exploited an instrumentalist logic; the policy was, she writes tellingly, 'manipulated' by various actors for various reasons (Nisbett 2013a: 11). In this case study, the richness of the interview material yields insights which could not be 'read off' from looking at the WCP itself – the backstory will have (inevitably) been tidied up or away. What this means, for some cultural policy analysts, is the need to shift away from a process perspective to one that instead explores practice and what Gray (2000: 4) sums up as 'the mundane, day-to-day activities of organizing, managing and funding' culture. Often this requires methodological mixing and attention to the object of enquiry from as many different perspectives as possible.

CULTURAL POLICY AS PRACTICE

An example which combines different methods and explores the coming together of discursive, textual, practical and experiential viewpoints can be found in the various outputs of a research project called The Meanings of the New Millennium Experience, which sought to analyse the Millennium Dome, built in Greenwich, London, as the site of the UK's millennium celebrations. Here we will focus on two contrasting publications arising from this project that approach the Dome in different ways, showing it in different lights. In 'Figuring out the Dome' (McGuigan and Gilmore 2001), the research draws extensively on official published data sources in order to compile the facts and statistics, sums of money and visitor data so as, in the words of its authors, to 'facilitate debate by providing reliable evidence' (41). With forensic attention to detail, this discussion presents exactly that – the story of the Dome as told by its official data. The tone throughout is (mainly) neutral and objective, a descriptive cataloguing of sponsorship, budgets, job creation and so on. While this might seem little more than an account of the mundane realities of cultural policy, there's an interesting subtext to 'Figuring out the Dome': it shows how public data on cultural projects can be assembled with relative ease – how the sector is, in fact, a major generator of research about itself. We see some familiar tools: MORI polls, annual reports, evaluations, impact studies. We want to pause for a moment to think about this, before heading back to the Dome.

One of the consequences of 'audit culture' and NPM has been a proliferation of data and documentation. In cultural policymaking, we can identify emerging methods from within the policy sector, therefore, as a crucial part of any analytical project. Earlier we nodded towards Mark Schuster's (2002) *Informing Cultural Policy*, a much-discussed book that maps out various forms of cultural data being produced by what he names the 'cultural policy research and information infrastructure' – national statistical agencies, government bodies and quangos, independent research institutes, networks and private consultancies, among others. What McGuigan and Gilmore do is to (seemingly) take the data produced around the Dome at face value, and re-present it in narrative form. At a time when, in other spheres of life, public statistical data is seen as under threat (BBC News 2012), one side effect of audit culture and NPM has been the *proliferation* of cultural data and statistics. In terms of the stories we are now able to uncover, therefore, we can follow the lead given here and 'figure out' many different cultural policies and projects.

But McGuigan and Gilmore are not only interested in facts and figures; in a second paper they focus on analysing the Dome itself, and explore the visitor experience (McGuigan and Gilmore 2002). This time, their toolkit does not just contain a pile of published data; it adds interviews, analysis of the Dome's 'contents', photographs and observational data, rounding out the story of the Millennium Dome via a self-described 'multidimensional analysis' (9). This means attending to the big discursive issues, via what they label as dialogical and ideological critique; this is also in part textual, exploring not only texts about the Dome but also the Dome-as-text, offering a reading of its contents grounded in knowledge of who 'wrote' it. But it also adds other 'readers', in terms of visitor experiences, and this is arguably one of the most revealing parts of the study. For what they found was an abundance of generosity, offsetting the cynicism that surrounded the Dome (for example, in much media coverage and critical comment). People enjoyed it (or, at least some of them did, some of the time). Moreover, McGuigan and Gilmore credit visitors with various degrees of 'reflexivity' – they did not simply buy into the official messages but made their own meanings. They too were 'figuring out' the Dome, on their own terms. Using a practice-oriented approach, then, the attention to detail that a single case study affords means that practice can be viewed in its many forms – the subtitle of their 2002 paper lists three: 'sponsoring, meaning and visiting'. This suggests an open-endedness to the Dome, more so perhaps than the accounting based purely on official facts and numbers. The Dome's story contains elements amenable to discourse, text, process and practice approaches, but perhaps it is only through multi-dimensional analysis that a fuller picture can be achieved. Of course, the worlds of policymaking and policy analysis are ever-turning, and we must scan the horizon for new things to study and new ways of studying. We end this chapter with one such turn.

NEW MOVES IN POLICY RESEARCH

Our use of the term 'new moves' is double, for our interest here is in the turn towards investigating 'policy mobilities'. While there has been a long-standing interest in 'policy transfer' – in the diffusion of policy ideas or wholesale policies from one location to another (Cairney 2012) – this new interest in policy's movements eschews the relatively simple model of diffusion/transfer and instead focusses on the different ways that policy travels. It's also interesting in that it requires researchers to pay close attention to 'the sites and situations where policy is assembled in practice' (Cochrane and Ward 2012: 9) and to the practices through which policy becomes mobile. Such a turn also necessitates new methods – mobile methods. Perhaps unsurprisingly, geographers have been at the forefront of theorising policy mobilities, drawing on ideas about relational geographies, flows and networks, morphing and mutation, notably in work on urban policy, including the 'viral spread of creative city policies' (Peck and Theodore 2010: 171; see also McCann and Ward 2011). A mobilities focus involves asking 'Who?' questions again, and researchers have identified a retinue of policy tourists and travellers, or 'policy peddlers and gurus' as Peck and Theodore (2010: 170) call them (themselves often also researching policy as they move it around). It also involves close attention to practice, to the mundane and daily business of making policy mobile: as McCann and Ward (2012: 45) write, 'staying "close to practice" ... necessitates detailed description and "tracing" of the travels, comparative techniques, and representational strategies, of policy actors who mobilise policy and engage with global circuits of policy knowledge'. To understand policy mobilities, therefore, they recommend methods that encourage 'following' – following people, policies and places as they 'move around'.

One example of such an approach is provided by Sara Gonzalez (2011) in her discussion of how Barcelona and Bilbao operate as sites for policy tourism. She intentionally chooses the term 'tourism' to signal some consonance between mobile policymakers' practices and experiences and those of leisure/recreational tourists, such as their shared dependence on myths about other places – and about the transformations that visiting such places can produce. She adds that policy tourism, 'like its leisure counterpart involves the rescripting of places, the reassembling of cities out of bits and pieces that are visited' (4). In her study, she accompanied and spoke with delegates from around the world, drawn to visit

Barcelona or Bilbao to learn from their 'success stories' in terms of culture-led regeneration, as well as talking to 'tour guides' and other 'locals' now servicing policy tourists. What Gonzalez's work points out is precisely the practices of policy mobility. In terms of cultural policy more broadly, there are clear examples of such mobility – creative industries policy is probably the best-known example (e.g. Luckman *et al*. 2009; Rantisi *et al*. 2006; Wang 2004). As we will examine further in later chapters, this partial deterritorialisation of policy is important at urban, national and global scales, reshaping the policy (and geographical) landscape in the process. When policies and policymakers are on the move, policy researchers need to be alive to the various flows that morph and mutate the objects of our study.

CONCLUSIONS

Our aim in this chapter has been to cast light on what 'policy' means in cultural policy and cultural policy research: to explore who makes policy, how it works, what it does, and how to study it. Clearly our review has been selective, but through the examples given we have plotted answers to these and other questions, reminding us that it is important not to treat cultural policy as a black box but to open the lid and look inside. The same is true for our own research: we need to think about how we approach cultural policy, what we understand it to be (and to be for), and therefore how we analyse it. Commentators often conclude that cultural policy research is at a crossroads – it is 'maturing' but simultaneously retaining an interdisciplinary heterogeneity. While this can make for heavy weather when trying to really get at what it is that cultural policy research is doing (and what it's doing it to), we have in this chapter tried to keep an open mind on the heterogeneity of the field, and indeed of the object of its study, while repeatedly underlining our key point: it is important to understand cultural policy as *policy*, as the outworking of ideas that take some sort of form, and as something that is assumed to produce effects – cultural policy is a doing. In the following chapters we think through this doing in more detail, deploying a scalar lens in order to carry on thinking through what cultural policy is.

REFERENCES AND FURTHER READING

Ahearne, J. (2009) 'Cultural policy explicit and implicit: a distinction and some uses', *International Journal of Cultural Policy*, 15(2): 141–53.

BBC News (2012) 'MPs warn census axing could harm social science'. Available at www.bbc.co.uk/news/uk-politics-19669695 (accessed 01/12/13).

Belfiore, E. (2004) 'Auditing culture: the subsidised cultural sector and the New Public Management', *International Journal of Cultural Policy*, 10(2): 183–202.

Bell, D. (2007) 'Fade to grey: some reflections on policy and mundanity', *Environment & Planning A*, 39(3): 541–54.

Bennett, O. (2004) 'The torn halves of cultural policy research', *International Journal of Cultural Policy*, 10(2): 237–48.

Bennett, T. (1998) *Culture: a Reformer's Science*, London: Sage.

Cairney, P. (2012) *Understanding Public Policy: Theories and Issues*, Houndmills: Palgrave.

Caust, J. (2003) 'Putting the "art" back into arts policymaking: how arts policy has been "captured" by the economists and the marketers', *International Journal of Cultural Policy*, 9(1): 51–63.

Cochrane, A. and Ward, K. (2012) 'Researching the geographies of policy mobility: confronting the methodological challenges', *Environment & Planning A*, 44(1): 5–12.

Craik, J., McAllister, L. and Davis, G. (2003) 'Paradoxes and contradictions in government approaches to contemporary cultural policy: an Australian perspective', *International Journal of Cultural Policy*, 9(1): 17–33.

DCMS (1999a) *Local Cultural Strategies*, London: DCMS.

——(1999b) *Regional Cultural Consortiums*, London, DCMS.

——(2000) *Creating Opportunities*, London: DCMS.

——(2004) *Guidance on Integrating Cultural and Community Strategies*, London: DCMS.

Dye, T. (2005) *Understanding Public Policy*, New York: Pearson.

Gilmore, A. (2004) 'Local cultural strategies: a strategic review', *Cultural Trends*, 13(3): 3–32.

Gonzalez, S. (2011) 'Bilbao and Barcelona "in motion": how urban regeneration 'models' travel and mutate in the global flows of policy tourism', *Urban Studies*, 48(7): 1397–418.

Gray, C. (2000) *The Politics of the Arts in Britain*, Basingstoke: Macmillan.

——(2004) 'Joining up or tagging on? The arts, cultural planning and the view from below', *Public Policy and Administration*, 19(2): 38–49.

——(2008) 'Instrumental policies: causes, consequences, museums and galleries', *Cultural Trends*, 17(4): 209–22.

——(2010) 'Analysing cultural policy: incorrigibly plural or ontologically incompatible?' *International Journal of Cultural Policy*, 16(2): 215–30.

Gray, C. and Wingfield, M. (2011) 'Are governmental culture departments important? An empirical investigation', *International Journal of Cultural Policy*, 17(5): 590–604.

Hesmondhalgh, D. (2005) 'Media and cultural policy as public policy: the case of the British Labour government', *International Journal of Cultural Policy*, 11(1): 95–109.

Hewison, R. (1995) *Culture and Consensus: England, Art and Politics since 1945*, London: Methuen.

Hunter, S. (2008) 'Living documents: a feminist psychosocial approach to the relational politics of policy documentation', *Critical Social Policy*, 28(4): 506–28.

Jowell, T. (2004) *Government and the Value of Culture*, London: DCMS.

Larson, G. (1997) *American Canvas*, Washington DC: NEA.

Lewis, J. and Miller, T. (eds) (2003) *Critical Cultural Policy Studies: A Reader*, London: Sage.

Looseley, D. (2011) 'Notions of popular culture in cultural policy: a comparative history of France and Britain', *International Journal of Cultural Policy*, 17(4): 365–79.

Luckman, S., Gibson, C. and Lea, T. (2009) 'Mosquitos in the mix: how transferable is creative city thinking?' *Singapore Journal of Tropical Geography*, 30(1): 70–85.

Magor, M. and Schlesinger, P. (2009) '"For this relief, much thanks": taxation, film policy and the UK government', *Screen*, 50(3): 299–317.

McCann, E. and Ward, K. (eds) (2011) *Mobile Urbanism: Cities and Policymaking in the Global Age*, Minneapolis MN: University of Minnesota Press.

McCann, E. and Ward, K. (2012) 'Assembling urbanism: following policies and "studying through" the sites and situations of policymaking', *Environment & Planning A*, 44(1): 42–51.

McGuigan, J. (2004) *Rethinking Cultural Policy*, Maidenhead: Open University Press.

——(2005) 'Neo-liberalism, culture and policy', *International Journal of Cultural Policy*, 11(3): 229–41.

McGuigan, J. and Gilmore, A. (2001) 'Figuring out the Dome', *Cultural Trends*, 39: 39–83.

——(2002) 'The Millennium Dome: sponsoring, meaning and visiting', *International Journal of Cultural Policy*, 8(1): 1–20.

Miller, T. and Yudice, G. (2002) *Cultural Policy*, London: Sage.

Mulcahy, K. (2006) 'Cultural policy', in B. Peters and J. Pierre (eds) *Handbook of Public Policy*, London: Sage.

Nisbett, M. (2013a) 'New perspectives on instrumentalism: an empirical study of cultural diplomacy', *International Journal of Cultural Policy*, 19(5): 557–75.

——(2013b) 'Protection, survival and growth: an analysis of international policy documents', *International Journal of Cultural Policy*, 19(1): 84–102.

Peck, J. and Theodore, N. (2010) 'Mobilizing policy: models, methods, and mutations', *Geoforum*, 41(2): 169–74.

Poirrier, P. (ed.) (2011) *La Culture Comme Politique Publique: essais d'histoire compare*, Paris: Documentation Francaise.

Pratt, A. (2005) 'Cultural industries and public policy: an oxymoron?' *International Journal of Cultural Policy*, 11(1): 31–44.

Rantisi, N., Leslie, D. and Christopherson, S. (2006) 'Placing the creative economy: scale, politics, and the material', *Environment and Planning A*, 38(10): 1789–97.

Royseng, S. (2008) 'The ritual logic of cultural policy', paper presented at the Fifth International Conference on Cultural Policy Research, Istanbul, 20–24 August. Available via www2.warwick.ac.uk (accessed 01/12/13).

Schuster, J. M. (2002) *Informing Cultural Policy: the Research and Information Infrastructure*, Brunswick NJ: Center for Urban Policy Research, SUNJ.

Scullion, A. and Garcia, B. (2005) 'What is cultural policy research?' *International Journal of Cultural Policy*, 11(2): 113–27.

Selwood, S. (2006) 'A part to play? The academic contribution to the development of cultural policy in England', *International Journal of Cultural Policy*, 12(1): 37–53.

Shore, C. and Wright, S. (eds) (1997) *Anthropology of Policy: Perspectives on Governance and Power*, London: Routledge.

Smith, C. (1998) *Creative Britain*, London: Faber & Faber.

Stevens, A. (2011) 'Telling policy stories: an ethnographic study of the use of evidence in policy-making in the UK', *Journal of Social Policy* 40(2): 237–55.

Stevenson, D., McKay, K. and Rowe, D. (2010) 'Tracing British cultural policy domains: contexts, collaborations and constituencies', *International Journal of Cultural Policy*, 16(2): 159–72.

Vestheim, G. (2012) 'Cultural policy-making: negotiations in an overlapping zone between culture, politics and money', *International Journal of Cultural Policy*, 18(5): 530–44.

Wallinger, M. and Warnock, M. (2000) (eds) *Art for All? Their Policies and Our Culture*, London: PEER.

Wang, J. (2004) 'The global reach of a new discourse: how far can "creative industries" travel?' *International Journal of Cultural Studies*, 7(1): 9–19.

Williams, R. (1984) 'State, culture and beyond', in L. Apignanesi (ed.) *Culture and the State*, London: ICA.

Worpole, K. (1998) 'Think-tanks, consultancies and urban policy in the UK', *International Journal of Urban and Regional Research*, 22(1): 147–55.

4

URBAN CULTURAL POLICY

Cultural policy is carried out at all levels of government, from supranational bodies such as the United Nations to local and neighbourhood levels. But perhaps the prime site of cultural policy development in the past thirty years or more has been the city. This chapter examines why that might be the case, the variety of ways in which cities develop and implement cultural policy, and the lessons we can learn from what is now an international body of research in urban cultural policy.

The first question to ask may seem an odd one: what is a city? Is it what many of us refer to as the 'city centre', the place where concert halls and museums, nightclubs and cinemas are often concentrated? Or is it the particular neighbourhoods of a city, which might have their own distinct cultural scenes? Is it where we live or where we work? Does it include suburbs or small towns, or is it just a few select centres with a strong cultural brand?

The question matters both for research and for policymakers. It is fair to say that, until recently, the majority of academic research on cultural policy for the city concentrated on large urban centres, particularly on what are sometimes termed 'World Cities' (Sassen 2006). This might be observed in a particularly magisterial way in Peter Hall's 1998 tome, *Cities in Civilisation*, in which he makes a grand, historic sweep of cities from ancient Athens to modern-day Los Angeles to seek to uncover the connection between cities, human creativity and innovation. Cities, he argues, are the motors of such creativity and innovation, and the reason they are is not just due to size, wealth or political power – though all that matters – but because they are open: open to new ideas, open to immigrants, open to different ways of life. It is this that he uses to answer his own, rather provocative question: 'why should the creative flame burn so especially, so uniquely, in cities and not in the countryside' (Hall 1998: 3)?

A number of contemporary writers would wish to take issue with this, and there has been recent growth in literature that looks at culture beyond the city: in suburbs, small towns and rural areas (Bell 2014; Bell and Jayne 2010; Luckman 2012; Thomas *et al.* 2013; Waitt and Gibson 2009). In part this results from what is seen as an over-concentration in cultural policy on a particular urban model, and concern that this marginalises too many communities and too many kinds of cultural activity, while valorising others. Some of the problems of urban cultural policy with which this chapter will deal, in particular the association between cultural developments and gentrification, seem to be worse in larger cities. In particular, there is growing evidence that larger cities are associated with greater levels of social inequality than smaller ones, particularly given housing cost pressures (Stolarick and Currid-Halkett 2013), and this has implications for artists and cultural producers of all sorts.

In addition (and obviously), cities are enormously heterogeneous spaces; difficult to summarise in one or two lines, despite the best efforts of the city-branding agencies. As emerges in our discussion of the nation (see Chapter 5), cities are imagined communities, narrating themselves in particular ways. Nichols Clark and Silver (2013: 28) give the example of Chicago, 'transforming its blue collar and localist heritage' into one that stresses public goods such as arts, entertainment and the heritage of its built environment. But such transformations can only ever be partial. As we shall see in this chapter; the city is also the site of conflict in cultural terms. Debates over identity, land and expression are often played out with particular ferocity on the urban stage, and many of the most contentious issues of cultural policy are urban in nature.

WHY CITIES?

While it now seems axiomatic that cities should be important hubs for both cultural activities and cultural policymaking, this has not always been the case. Indeed, Grodach and Silver (2013) argue that urban cultural policy is a relatively new concept, dating back around thirty years, before which culture was largely a matter for the nation-state. The coming to prominence of the city in cultural policy parallels its role in the global discourse of the 'knowledge-based economy', as urban economies have been restructured around business and consumer services, with a corresponding growth in employment in the cultural sectors. As a result,

> A global network of cities have made determined efforts to capture these fast growing, high human capital sectors with a range of policy programs that tend to be guide by neoliberal deregulation and privatisation and a reframing of traditional progressive policy goals such as diversity, inclusion, quality of life and sustainability, as facets of urban growth.
>
> (Grodach and Silver 2013: 3)

Yet this process was not inevitable. The city in the post-war years, particularly in the USA and parts of Europe, became associated with a series of social and economic problems including crime, poor housing and over-stretched social services (MacLennan and Norman 2004). This restructuring created highly differentiated cities and parts of cities, privileging some economic sectors and types of employment (Massey 2007). This in turn led to a concentration of economically deprived households in some inner-city neighbourhoods, as prosperous households moved out in a general shift of population from urban areas to suburbs, market towns and rural locations.

Conventional wisdom at the time was that cities were in for a long period of decline as those who could – often better-educated, more mobile workers – would leave for the suburbs. The assumption was that this phenomenon would be facilitated by the growth of digital technology, heralding a future of geographic dispersal and telecommuting (Cairncross 1997; Coyle 1997). Place, it was said, had become unimportant.

In fact the reverse has happened. Urbanisation, a feature of modernity across the world, is continuing at unprecedented rates, and the majority of the world's population now lives in cities (United Nations 2011). And far from being seen by policymakers as the source of all problems, cities are often heralded as the source of all solutions. As one report from the UK government put it: 'Our cities are back: competitive cities make prosperous regions and sustainable communities' (ODPM 2004: 1).

And if cities have become more important to policy overall, culture has become more important to cites. This is not entirely new. The relationship between spatial configuration and economic activity has been understood at least since Alfred Marshall coined the phrase 'industrial district' to describe, among other activities, steelmaking in the nineteenth century (Marshall 1925). But the relationship between place and culture is not just about economic production. The city had traditionally been seen as a refuge for those seeking a new life; as the old Germanic saying has it, 'city air makes you free'. The 'bohemia' of nineteenth-century Paris saw artists and intellectuals locate in neighbourhoods such as the Latin Quarter or Montparnasse, which became associated with what would later be referred to as an alternative or counter-culture (Hall 1998). Some of these neighbourhoods also became magnets for migrants or refugees. London's East End, which was once settled by Huguenot weavers escaping religious persecution in France, has subsequently been host to communities of Jewish, Bangladeshi and Polish migrants, as well as to a fluctuating community of artists and craft workers (Oakley and Pratt 2010).

Cities have also been the traditional location of our grandest cultural inheritances – from the Gothic cathedral to the contemporary art gallery. European countries such as Germany or Italy have the heritage of former cities that once held autonomous political power and still have the built environment to prove it; think Sienna, Avignon or Heidelberg. Even what remains to us of the built environment of far older civilisations often manifests itself in an urban form, as in Damascus or Cairo. And although there are great art collections in country houses, chateaux and churches, the majority of 'national' art collections are displayed, with great pride, in major cities across the world.

Thus, it is not just that cultural activities are concentrated in the urban conurbation but that much of their 'support infrastructure' is inseparable from that of the city. The things that contribute to a vibrant cultural sector are part of the wider cultural assets of a city, its sense of identity, its record shops, its large and small venues, its libraries and book shops, its museums and galleries, its parks and open spaces, its schools and universities, students and cafés.

The primary drivers of cultural investment at the urban scale in recent decades have been economic: the cultural sectors are seen as source of jobs and growth, they are seen to make cities more attractive to outside investors, mobile workers and tourists. The other rationale for cultural funding, its role in improving the quality of life and social sustainability of cities, is frequently evoked in urban cultural policy but rarely seem to be *driving* cultural policy in the city. Problems occur, as we shall see, when polices designed to develop the economic assets of a city's culture pay insufficient attention to these other criteria, or deliberately promote interventions that may harm the delicate ecosystem that underpins a city's culture. Conflicts often arise, for example when the successful development of cultural consumption spaces makes rental charges unsustainable for cultural producers, or more generally as cities following a 'creative' development path have become notably more socially unequal (Florida 2013).

The problem for policymakers is that these deep and interlinking assets are only occasionally the results of deliberate *cultural* policy. They are much more often the legacy of education policy, transport policy, planning and licensing laws, migration and housing policy, of philanthropy and commercial hard sell – mixed together with a variety of cultural assets, public and private. So complex is this mix that policymakers often seem to fall back on a 'toolbox' approach to urban cultural policymaking, driven, as Grodach and Silver (2013) describe above, by a similar set of political understandings and policy approaches. The next section describes some of the interventions that are common in urban cultural policymaking.

CULTURAL POLICIES IN THE CITY

FLAGSHIP CULTURAL BUILDING AND REGENERATION

Mention culture and the city in the same breath and the image that might spring to many minds is Frank Gehry's spectacular, wave-like design for the Guggenheim Museum in Bilbao, northern Spain. Opening in 1997, the Bilbao Guggenheim was far from the first of such projects, but has come to symbolise a particular and highly influential approach to 'culturally led regeneration'. In particular, it brings together a declining industrial city, huge public investment, a globally famous architect, an iconic building and an association with 'high culture' in a formula for urban revitalisation that has been much replicated and much criticised.

As García (2004) points out, the legacy of the Barcelona Olympics and the Seville Expo meant that Spain in the early 1990s saw urban regeneration very much as an outcome of flagship, high-profile capital projects. The Guggenheim – a cultural icon in a depressed, post-industrial city – fitted this picture exactly and was joined by other major infrastructure projects in the city, notably a high-quality subway system designed by Norman Foster. As she suggests, the short-term benefits were impressive: a worldwide transformation of the city's image, indicated by a large rise in tourism. Overseas tourism was up 42.7 per cent between 1994 and 2000 and Spanish tourism up even more, by 58 per cent.

But in recent years questions have been asked about the sustainability of such high-profile initiatives. As David Harvey argued over two decades ago, despite their relatively high costs, such flagship projects can in fact be relatively easily reproduced in different locations, 'thus rendering any competitive advantage within a system of cities ephemeral' (Harvey [1989a] 2000: 361). In Bilbao's case, the large rise in tourism was not sustained, though arguably the image of the city was permanently altered. Yet there was little evidence of wider economic benefits beyond tourism, and while a series of wider urban regeneration projects were also undertaken, the sheer scale of the Guggenheim investment – estimated as some 144 million Euros – meant that the contrast between the 'favoured' area and the surrounding neighbourhoods appeared stark. Brenda Yeoh (2005) argues that similar problems are arising in Southeast Asia where, she claims, 'the use of cultural imagineering, urban mega-projects and iconic architecture' in urban regeneration is even more spatially concentrated, widening the gap between those cities that see themselves as global players and those 'at the bottom of the hierarchy which are perceived to be structurally irrelevant to the current round of global capital accumulation' (Yeoh 2005: 955).

Partly because large-scale projects are intended to serve national or international populations, they may produce mixed feelings among local people and local cultural producers. Graeme Evans (2004) argues that this lack of a link between flagship cultural projects and local creative businesses is not confined to Bilbao but is a weakness of similar schemes everywhere. Indeed, he goes on to argue, along with others (Hannigan 1998; Kong 2012), that such flagship projects are often undertaken *at the expense of* local and regional cultural development, siphoning off funds that could have been used to support local cultural industries.

Nonetheless, the perceived success of Bilbao, what some have dubbed the 'Bilbao effect', led to a number of other cities seeking to follow suit (Gonzalez 2011). While the growth of global architectural firms and 'starchitects' such as Gehry was already in train by the 1990s (Sudjic 1993), the linking of such signature buildings to particular cultural 'brands' takes this process even further. The Guggenheim Foundation in particular, under then-Director Thomas Krens, began a global expansion, with planned openings in Taiwan, Mexico, Brazil and the UEA, as well as extensions to its existing institutions in New York and Venice. A combination of adverse financial conditions, local resistance and organisational over-reaching has seen many of these projects fail, notably in Rio where the proposed Jean Nouvel-designed Guggenheim was halted after a series of legal challenges alleging that city authorities had exceeded their power in agreeing to ten years of payments to the Guggenheim Foundation (Yudice 2009). Planned schemes for Guadalajara, Mexico and Taichung, Taiwan were cancelled even earlier in the process (Ponzini 2013).

Despite setbacks for Guggenheim and the general chilling of large architectural projects since the start of the global financial crisis in 2008, this particular approach to urban cultural policy is not completely exhausted. Abu Dhabi's Saadiyat Island development, which includes an outpost of the Louvre defined by Jean Nouvel, Zahia Hadid's performing arts centre, Tadao Ando's Maritime Museum and Norman Foster's Sheikh Zahad National Museum, both exemplifies this approach and reflects many of its shortcomings. To a greater extent even than Bilbao, the Saadiyat Island developments represent the importance of cultural brands, in the case of both architects and institutions such as the Louvre. Despite the stated aim of architects such as Gehry and Nouvel to reflect what they see as elements of traditional Arab towns in their design, the lack of connection between such high-profile investments and local cultural practice is striking. Elsheshtawy (2012) argues that while steps have been taken to counter the perception of cultural colonialism, including a series of seminars, exhibitions and art fairs designed to produce a 'museum-going population' in the region, it is difficult to escape the view that the intended audience is in fact international investors and tourists.

A characteristic of the development in Abu Dhabi, reflected in other developments such as the Guggenheim in Rio (Yudice 2009), is the lack of consultation with local cultural institutions or artists and, in some cases, the bypassing of local planning procedures (Ponzini 2013). A result of this, alongside distrust and disengagement, is that rather than reinforcing the distinctiveness of cities, the homogenising effects of global architectural imprints, along with global retail and consumption offers, tends to weaken any sense of place, ironically weakening their appeal to 'discerning' consumers.

CULTURAL QUARTERS AND CLUSTERS

While high-profile galleries and museums are sometimes the centrepiece of cultural or artistic districts within cities, there is another tradition of more localised development, often focussed on supporting production, which can be seen in contrast to the Bilbao model. Known variously as cultural quarters, clusters or districts, these different types of development draw their primary orientation from distinct policy drivers: those devoted to cultural production from artists' studios to managed workspace for high-tech start-ups; those devoted to consumption and leisure such as MuseumQuartier in Vienna or Prymont-Ultimo in Sydney; and those which focus on local regeneration or community development. However, in practice, many cultural or creative quarters take on multiple roles over time, with cultural workspace often giving way to residential or consumption uses.

The quintessential example of this – the redevelopment of SoHo, New York in the 1980s captured by Sharon Zukin (1982) in *Loft Living* – was originally artist-driven, with large windows in former industrial buildings providing good light and lifts designed for freight being used to transport canvasses. Other cities such as Philadelphia, Paris, Berlin and Stockholm have seen artist-led organisations take over former industrial spaces and provide subsidised or at least stable rent to artists (Evans 2001).

As manufacturing industries abandoned many European city centres, traditional workspaces were repurposed as lofts or studios, with artists or craft workers taking over former warehouses. In some cases, the new arrivals represent a completely new industry: videogames where meatpackers once worked, for example. In other cases, such as an area historically associated with garment manufacture, there may be an attempt to build on this legacy with more specialist 'higher-end' craft work: within the UK, for example, this is the case in Nottingham's Lace Market area or Birmingham's Jewellery Quarter (Crewe and Beaverstock 1998).

The evidence suggests that most cultural industries are biased in favour of the urban; that is, cultural industries are more likely to be found within cities, particularly large cities, and indeed are often part of the 'brand image' of a city. Think of Milan and fashion, Paris and fine art, or Los Angeles and filmmaking. Of course, these high-profile cases are the exception rather than the rule and some industries are only present in a few cities around the world (Scott 2000, 2005; Scott and Power 2004), but the success of these world centres is enough to persuade policymakers in much smaller cities to take an interest in developing the cultural industries.

Much of the work on developing the cultural industries within cities has used Michael Porter's (1998) notion of 'clusters' along with related ideas such as the 'industrial district' and 'innovative milieu' to try and develop the cultural sector (O'Connor 2004; Pratt 2000). Porter's idea, which some have argued is ill-suited to the cultural industries (Pratt 2002), simply refers to the co-location of interconnected business, suppliers and relevant institutions in particular industrial sectors. In the cultural sectors, the tendency to co-locate, sometimes within a few city streets, is driven by the need for cultural producers to swap ideas and contacts, socialise together and trade industry gossip (Currid 2007; Lloyd 2006; Pratt 2006). This is sometimes referred to as 'tacit knowledge exchange', based on Michael Polanyi's (1966) famous assertion that we know more than we can tell. Tacit knowledge refers to the kind of informal knowledge that is difficult to codify. If we think about the process of cultural production, artists, writers and musicians are often employing an informal 'feel' for what people might want, combined with a personal need for expression.

Communicating these ideas is best done face to face, even in activities such as advertising or videogames production that make much use of digital technology (Pratt 2011). Indeed, research suggests that the higher up the value chain – and the closer to the creative elements of production – the more likely it is that face-to-face interaction will be important (Pratt 2006, 2011). While this is true of other 'knowledge-based sectors' – the trading and investment activities of the financial services industry also tend to cluster, for example – the urban co-location of cultural activities also owes something to the urban environment itself. Opportunities for cultural consumption are generally greater in cities than elsewhere, and the link between production and consumption is often strong. Musicians are generally keen consumers of music, for example. Moreover, the exchange of ideas on which cultural production thrives is commonly found in an interpenetration of the formal and informal, commercial and non-commercial fields in which cities are rich: public art galleries combined with street art, subsidised theatre alongside commercial shows.

In some cities there are reputational effects where they have become associated with certain 'scenes', as in the case of Sheffield, Bogota or Detroit and popular music, and this can create a virtuous circle whereby people interested in a cultural practice are drawn to these cities. For firms in the cultural industries, and for the associated leisure sectors from bars and clubs to coffee shops and independent retail, being located in certain areas can be invested with what is sometimes referred to as 'symbolic capital' (Currid 2007; Harvey [1989a] 2000; Lloyd 2006). This symbolic capital is sometimes difficult for other cities to reproduce. Moloch (1976: 229) describes it as a ' a kind of monopoly rent that adheres to places', which can create barriers to the reception of products from other places or enable producers within certain cities – Milan fashion houses, for example – to charge a premium.

Despite the success of some cities in developing a strong cultural-industry base in one or more sectors, these developments often prove difficult for city authorities to control and, as in the case of the flagship cultural developments described above, successful cultural clusters can be associated with processes of gentrification. As in New York's SoHo district, these spaces of production have, over time, been captured by high-end retail and consumption activities and rising rents which make them unsuitable for either relatively low-paid cultural workers or the poorer communities that once formed part of their social mix.

CITY COMPETITIONS

The growing importance of culture for cities is reflected in a growth in city 'competitions', not just for mega-events such as the Olympics or expos, but also to become 'Capital of Culture' – these competitions are now being fought in Asia as well as Europe (see Chapter 6). In addition there are numerous competitions for 'City of Design', 'Literature', 'Film' and so on, which have not only influenced and in some cases redirected cultural policy and resources but also reinforced the tendency towards a toolkit-type approach to urban cultural policy.

Such events have multiple audiences: within the city itself, nationally and internationally, though the prime focus differs across cities. Liverpool's year as European Capital of Culture in 2008 was said to have improved its image as a city, though arguably those perceived image problems were more likely to exist within the UK than they were internationally. Beijing used the Olympics in

2008 to confirm China's growing power and influence both with an international audience and within its own borders.

Although one of the older forms of urban mega-events, tracing their origins back to nineteenth-century world's fairs (Roche 1998), expos have seen something of a revival in recent decades, confirmed by Shanghai's successful hosting of the 2010 Expo, two years after the Beijing Olympics. Shanghai's Expo site was by far the largest that has ever been built and the combination of its policy of funding the participation of poorer nations, as well as its pulling power as a trade partner – the EU as an entity broke with its policy of not attending expos that take place outside the EU for the first time – meant that its expo succeeded in cementing the image of Shanghai as a major world city.

Although not strictly speaking a cultural festival, by celebrating design and architecture via the pavilions, expos can be seen as a form of 'culture as display' in the same way that sporting events like the Olympics are, now accompanied by very large cultural festivals, as was the case in 2012 in London. Beatriz García (2004) has questioned the relationship between mega-events – even ones with a strong cultural theme – and the development of sustainable arts and culture within a city. In her case study of three mega-events in three cities (Glasgow's year as City of Culture in 1990, the Sydney Olympics Arts Festival in 2000, and Barcelona's 2004 Universal Forum for Cultures), García points out that all the cities put arts at the centre of their bid to host these events. Such an emphasis is likely to be used within bids to suggest a strong social or community focus for the event and allay concerns that it is simply about attracting international tourists or business investment. But once the bid is won and the event developed, in many cases arts programming becomes more marginal: 'these programmes are frequently excluded from the event's mainstream promotions and receive insufficient funding to address defined objectives' (García 2004: 114). Even within a cultural festival like 'Capital of Culture', the emphasis may be on large one-off cultural events, whether Ringo Starr or Pavarotti, rather than more local or more innovative work. Good relationships with the local arts scene are often developed during the bidding process but these are often not sustained over the longer term.

The criticism that García makes here of mega-events points to a potential weakness of many of the policy initiatives described above. As the traditional home of the high points of world culture, the city often seems to concern itself with the spectacular, the grand and the cosmopolitan, using culture to make a statement to the wider world. The failing of many such policies, whether flagship buildings, mega-events or cultural quarters, is their lack of integration with the more demotic, everyday cultural life of the city. Fragmentation, short-termism and elitism are some of the criticisms that are made of these policies, and it was partly to address these failings that the 'creative city' paradigm was originally conceived.

THE CREATIVE CITY

The term 'creative city' is now so widely used (and abused) in discussions of urban cultural policy that it has become a shorthand term in policy discourse for contemporary ideas about culture and the city and in more critical discourse for the problems of urban cultural development. There are a number of cities which brand themselves as 'creative' and a number of creative city networks, including ones organised by UNESCO,[1] national groupings such as the Creative Cities Network of Canada[2] and those run by private sector consultants. Gibson refers to this discourse simply as the 'conventional creative city script' (Gibson 2013: 125), though Pratt (2012) notes that there have always been various versions of the creative city idea, not all of which conform to the same 'script'.

Indeed, the original notion of the creative city was addressed as much to questions of how policymaking is done as it was to the object of that policy (Landry 2000; Landry and Bianchini 1995). Creativity in this context referred to the need to have a more self-conscious and reflexive process of thinking about the city, not simply about the 'creative' sectors of its economy, thus avoiding some of the problems referred to above. Essential to this was the idea of cultural planning: the requirement to integrate cultural needs into *all* aspects of the urban policymaking process, from public transport to arts education in schools, rather than simply using culture as a tool of economic development (Mercer 2002). Vital for cultural planning as well as for similar notions that go by names such as 'creative placemaking' (Markusen and Gadwa 2010) is the involvement of agencies outside the cultural sphere, in fields from transport to health, and with professionals from architects to psychologists, as well as citizens and community representatives. It is in fact more of a method of policymaking than a policy per se.

The need to address social fragmentation, fear and alienation in urban communities and develop what could be regarded as a distinctive sense of place was thus part of the original creative city 'script', though it is an aspect which many of the later incarnations of this idea downplayed. Landry and Bianchini's (1995) original model of the 'creative city' pays as much attention to the role of culture in ameliorating the social problems of a city as to its role in boosting economic prospects (though the degree to which these elements may be in conflict, for example in culturally led gentrification, is not fully addressed in their work).

The idea of 'policy transfer' is important in Landry and Bianchini's work on the creative city and policy ideas from Barcelona, Helsinki, Melbourne and elsewhere are described. These were as wide-ranging as winter festivals in Helsinki, the redevelopment of vacant industrial space in the Ruhr or centres for recycling and eco-technology in Copenhagen. Such notions of good or innovative practice were held up as models for other cities to adopt. Somewhat ironically, given Landry and Bianchini's stress on the importance of distinct, local approaches, the 'creative city' itself became one such idea, exemplifying Peck's notion of 'fast policy' whereby policy ideas are rapidly transferred from one jurisdiction to another via networks of specialist consultants and policy advisors, often without sufficient concern for the local political or economic situation (Peck 2004, 2005; see also Chapter 3).

Rather than the more sophisticated idea of policy mobility, Pratt (2009) describes how the unthinking transfer of the creative city idea can actually hamper efforts to really think about and engage with a localised set of conditions and opportunities, with policymakers instead preferring to adopt what he calls a 'Xerox' approach of policy copying. This is not to say that once ideas touch down in particular cities or regions they are not adapted and changed; they often are. Kong *et al.* (2006) have described how the discourse of the 'creative economy' was absorbed, but also altered, in the case of Hong Kong, Singapore, South Korea and Taiwan. City size, location and policy coalitions make a difference, as Waitt and Gibson (2009) have also described in their account of the development of cultural policies in the relatively small Australian city of Wollongong. But in the case of the creative city, fast policy transfer often meant that the idea, developed in the context of a de-industrialising Europe, arrived shorn of any of its social concerns, turned into a 'recipe' for the successful economic development of creative cities often in very different circumstances (O'Connor 2009; UNESCO 2013). Part of this recipe was undoubtedly the development of cultural tourism and entertainment and leisure facilities, to which we will now turn.

THE CITY AS AN ATTRACTION

Rather than focussing on the growth of cultural production, culture in this context is used as spectacle to attract inward investment, cultural tourism or skilled workers. Tourism is an obvious example of this phenomenon, visible in globally famous tourist attractions such as the pyramids at Giza, Angkor Wat or the Eiffel Tower. Some of such attractions are urban, like the canals of Venice or the temples of Kyoto. This type of symbolic capital is obviously more difficult to mimic – no one is replicating Venice's cityscape anytime soon – but it is also vulnerable to its own success. Large numbers of tourists can have the effect of deterring other tourists; the aesthetic or spiritual resonances of the Sistine Chapel are difficult for all but the most determined to detect above the noise of the crowd.

But what of the majority of cities, which while they have their own, local and distinctive culture may not make it into the top tier of global tourist attractions? They too have been seeking how to market and develop their own cultural assets and 'brands'. From the 1970s onwards, city authorities have sought to develop what they variously called arts or entertainment districts. A classic and much-examined case of this is the redevelopment of Baltimore

Harbour in the USA, which sought to combine cultural 'experience' with other consumption activities like shopping, restaurants and bars, partly to attract tourists and partly as a way of attracting middle-class residents back to city centres (Hannigan 1998; Harvey 1989b). The redeveloped waterfront is now so much part of the urban experience (at least for those cities with waterfronts) that it is difficult to imagine a time when rivers where simply regarded as transport systems on which cities often turned their backs.

Other strategies have focussed on developing what one might call more 'street level' cultural attractions, or working on the 'liveability' of cities, such as providing good access to green space or bike lanes. Although these can clearly be of benefit to existing citizens, such schemes are often justified, and indeed financed, as a way of attracting and retaining well-paid professional labour. The work of Richard Florida (2002) is a well-known example of this type of approach. Because of his idea of the 'creative class', a loose grouping of professional and knowledge workers, Florida has become associated with the discourse of creative cities more generally. But his strategy for economic development is built around talent attraction – in Florida's work generally the attraction of high-tech workers and industries – not the growth of the cultural industries themselves.

Florida's contribution to thinking in this area was to link the insights of urbanists (Hall 1998; Jacobs 1961) and 'new growth theorists' (Romer 1994) about the importance of skilled labour and the roles of cities in attracting that labour to the mobility of skilled workers, who he terms 'the creative class'. Florida argues that these people will pursue employment opportunities less for the qualities of the job itself and more for the amenities and lifestyle options – including cultural facilities – of the city or region where jobs are located.

Many cities around the world have adopted a 'Floridian' template for urban development (Berry 2005; Boyle 2006; Hui et al. 2004; Kong et al. 2006), but Florida's work has been heavily criticised by other scholars (see Oakley 2009 for a summary) on grounds both empirical and political. Perhaps the most stinging critiques of Florida's work have been those that have concentrated on the potential social consequences of a Floridian urban strategy. Critics have accused him of legitimising gentrification and of paying insufficient attention to the issues of inequality and racial discrimination (Markusen 2005; Peck 2005; Scott 2006). Others argue that Florida's urban policy prescriptions are not only insufficiently attuned to the problems of inequality but actively promote them. In terms of public spending on culture, for example, Florida's preference for street-level culture means that resources may be made available for certain kinds of cultural consumption (restaurants, bars, nightclubs, a music scene), while others (such as historic buildings) may be neglected. While funding for cultural amenities has always reflected certain kinds of taste preferences (traditionally high art over popular culture), an over-concentration on the amenities that attract the young or bohemian at the expense of others could be counterproductive as well as undemocratic.

It is clear that focussing attention on the actions and investments needed to attract the creative class may well lead to a neglect of other policies, from affordable childcare and good schools to public transport that may apply to older or poorer citizens or female workers. Similarly, the mobile, those who can and do move around for work or for leisure purposes, are preferred to older, poorer citizens who are less likely to be mobile. The 'non-creative' class are thus marginalised twice; once because their consumption preferences and needs do not reflect those of the creative class, and secondly because the effect of an influx of the creative class may well raise land and housing prices and drive out the provision of more basic services (Massey 2007).

Rapidly growing inequality is a disturbing feature of many cities around the world, whether they have adopted a 'creative class' route to development or not. But the criticism aimed at creative city advocates is that they often present a much more balanced and inclusive model of urban life than their policies actually produce. When that does happen, a less optimistic picture of the creative economy appears; in the USA at least, city-regions that rank highest in terms of creative economic strength also rank highest in economic inequality. As Florida suggests, rather meekly, 'on close inspection, talent clustering provides little in the way of trickle-down benefits' (Florida 2013: 1).

In response to this, some city governments have sought to take a more pro-active stance to ensure that culturally led economic development is more balanced and less in danger of driving out the artists and other locals on which it depends. Stuart Cameron and Jon Coaffee (2005) in their study of Gateshead in the northeast of England argue that there is a distinction between cities where gentrification is driven by commercial capital and those where what they call 'positive gentrification' is driven by public authorities, though in many cases public authorities lack legislative tools to combat rent rises and the change of use from production to consumption in 'successful' neighbourhoods.

Alongside the push to develop the cultural industries within cities and use culture for urban competiveness, the city has also been the site of active resistance on the part of artists and activists to contemporary cultural/economic policies. We discuss this further below, but it is also worth noting that alongside unsustainable cultural developments, a variety of cities have been attempting to embed cultural activity within policies aimed at ensuring that cities remain 'liveable' and sustainable.

URBAN AND SOCIAL SUSTAINABILITY

As discussed in Chapter 3, the idea that cultural policy, and cultural spending, can play some sort of role in addressing questions of social inequality is part of what Royseng calls its 'ritual logic' (Royseng 2008). Within the context of urban cultural policy, culture has often been harnessed to social objectives, whether in terms of specific goals such as reducing reoffending rates or improving the educational attainments of schoolchildren (Bamford 2006), or more for general aims such as promoting 'liveability' or social inclusion and community cohesion (see also Chapter 3). The exact role of culture within these processes is sometimes difficult to determine, particularly given the evidence that culturally-led economic development can also produce social polarisation. However, research, much of which has taken place in Canada and the USA, indicates that participating in cultural and creative activities helps build connections between people, sometimes referred to as 'social capital', including people from different backgrounds (Markusen and Gadwa 2010a; Stern and Seifert 2010).

Mark Stern and Susan Seifert's work (2000, 2010) suggests that neighbourhood effects have some role to play in determining who will participate in cultural activities. In particular, density of cultural activities, particularly very locally, means that people who live in such neighbourhoods are more likely to participate in cultural activities; in contrast to some other researchers, they argue that those who live in neighbourhoods that are more diverse (economically and ethnically) have higher rates of cultural participation than those in more homogeneous urban neighbour-hoods. Their conclusion is that cultural participation 'needs to be seen as a form of collective behaviour' (Stern and Seifert 2000: 6), and thus that attempts to encourage cultural participation should be aimed at neighbourhoods, by improving community-level cultural facilities, rather than at individuals. Jeannotte (2003a, 2003b) argues that those who participate in cultural activities are more likely to volunteer in other capacities. This finding is supported by Bourdeau (2002), who argues that this remains solid even after controlling for socio-economic and demographic factors such as gender, income and education. Other researchers suggest that participation in cultural events has more influence than participation in other kinds of events when it comes to developing various elements of social capital such as trust and tolerance (Stolle and Rochon, 1998).

As even Robert Puttnam, one of the primary advocates of the benefits of social capital admits, however, 'the causal arrows among civic involvement, reciprocity, honesty and social trust are as tangled as well tossed spaghetti' (Putnam 2000: 38). Add culture to the mix and it gets even more complicated. In other words, data on association is strong, but we are no closer to understanding if there is a *causal* link between participation in cultural activities and trusting other people; or what the nature of that link would be.

Well-being is another area of public policy which has recently attracted the attention of cultural policymakers and, despite a relatively large amount of research in this field, similar issues arise. In 2010 the UK government reported on a three-year research programme, the Culture and Sport Evidence Programme (CASE), which looked at both the drivers and impacts of participation in sport and cultural activity. A key strand of the programme was to understand and assess the improvements in subjective well-being generated by doing sport and engaging with culture (CASE 2010).

The researchers found some support for the argument that participating in sporting or cultural activities could have benefits in terms of how people feel about their lives, but the research was unable to determine what kind of cultural activities might lead to well-being benefits, thus there was little to help cultural policy-makers allocate funds. Before policymakers rush to prescribe 'more culture' as the cure for social ills, we need to better understand *whose* culture we are talking about. The long-standing debates between supporters of 'high art' and 'popular culture', between public and private investments and old and new cultural institutions is given fresh perspective by the argument that culture feeds into and can influence levels of social well-being.

As Abigail Gilmore (2013) has commented, much of the research on cultural activities, even at the local level, looks at people's inclination to take part in 'recognised' art or cultural activities, rather than starting from what people actually do in their spare time. When policy shifts its focus to looking at what people actually do, it may be that categories such as 'users' and 'nonusers' of culture become more complex or even fade away, leaving policy to concentrate on funding a diverse mix of activities, particularly at a highly localised level.

While most urban cultural policy focusses on participating in culture in the sense of symbolic activities, another strand of thinking looks at culture in the 'anthropological' sense and asks to what extent and how people from different religious and ethnic backgrounds can learn to live together within the city. In cities throughout the world this situation is made more complex by the position of ethnic and religious minorities as migrants in a different (and dominant) culture. Migrant communities tend to be concentrated in cities, so questions of multiculturalism and interculturalism are often the concern of urban policymakers as well as national ones.

Multiculturalism as a policy construct in the UK began as a response to the 'assimilationist' approach of the 1960s and 1970s, and sought to recognise the distinct cultural traditions of migrant communities and their British-born descendants. Urban cultural policy has sometimes sought to support and celebrate these different communities, branding particular areas of cities with an ethnic identity, like Banglatown in London's East End, or numerous Chinatowns and Little Italies (Kunnemann and Mayer 2013). More recent thinking has focussed on the ideas of 'interculturalism', which stresses the multiplicity of identities that we all have, rather than seeking to 'fix' an identity for an individual or community (Fanshawe and Sriskandarajah 2010). In terms of cultural policy, this suggests the need to create spaces and occasions for encounter, communication and shared activities between communities, what Hajer and Reijndorp (2001: 11) call the new public domain, 'where exchange between different social groups is possible'. For that they argue we need to move our gaze away from purely traditional spaces of culture – the main square, the art gallery, the concert hall – and acknowledge that public transport, the street and the park, the shopping mall and the airport are also places of culture (Wood and Landry 2008).

URBAN POLICY COALITIONS

Development of urban cultural policy involves not only local government but also non-governmental actors such as cultural industry employers, arts organisations, citizens' groups and property developers. This is part of a wider trend towards decentralised government or 'governance', sharpened by the idea of cities 'competing' in a global system for resources, jobs and investment. The combination of symbolic, aesthetic and economic cultural activities which cities are rich in has been harnessed by a variety of local governments, in a process that Harvey ([1989a] 2000) describes as 'urban entrepreneurialism'.

As city governments increasingly focus on economic development as a priority, cities seek to use their cultural assets in competition for people and resources, as we have seen. This idea of 'competitiveness', not just for businesses, but for cities, is fundamentally misguided according to some commentators (Buck et al. 2005). But the metaphor of competition serves to suggest that economic success is the major criterion by which cities should be judged, and despite the growth of city 'rankings' which consider other aspects of urban life, from liveability to cultural assets (Mayor of London 2013), the dominant logic is that cities should see themselves as acting more like firms, complete with brands, marketing departments and public relations staff. Yet, as we have seen, this pursuit of economic competiveness often comes into conflict with cultural or social aspirations, and the process of coalition-building around cultural policy is often conflicted and contentious.

As cultural policy has become more high profile within cities, the ability of cultural policymakers − traditionally concerned with arts and leisure provision rather than economic development − to respond to increasing demands has been questioned (O'Connor and Gu 2013). A particular concern is that planning legalisation, which many would argue is the key to sustainable cultural development, is generally outside the remit of 'cultural' policymakers (Grodach and Silver 2013). Yet many of the most important decision concerning culture − workspace for artists, rents, zoning and land-use planning, licensing and regulation of the night-time economy − are in the domain of planners who may or may not work in consultation with cultural policymakers. Often cultural policymakers lack the legislative tools to be able to enforce 'pro-culture' policies, even if the nature of such policies can be easily agreed on.

Elected leaders can also play an important role in the cultural profile of city. A few, including Ken Livingstone in London, Antanas Mockus in Bogota, Richard M. Daley in Chicago, have been associated with particular approaches to cultural policymaking (Nichols Clark and Silver 2013; Oakley 2013; Pasotti 2013). These can lean towards the large and spectacular, a high-profile gallery or museum opening, but may, as in Livingstone's 'cultural industry' policies or Mokus' 'citizen culture', be built around the notion of a more democratic cultural landscape within the city. But other elected officials have seen arts or cultural programmes as 'soft' services, first in line for public spending cuts.

Different cities will have different policy coalitions surrounding culture; larger arts institutions are more important in some cities than others, for example, while some cities have a stronger heritage of third-sector or community provision. Yet in almost all cities property developers have become an important policy player. This is a particular challenge for cities where cultural policymaking capacity and legislation is generally weak or has been weakened by a deregulatory policy regime. The dominance of property developer interests often centred on the development of city centre spaces with strong retail and leisure interests has been studied in a number of cities (Markusen and Gadwa 2010a; Zukin 1995). In a few cases, active mayors or arts and citizen groups have been able to resist or modify developer influence (Silver 2013), but the general trend has been toward a strong focus on city centres and particular neighbourhoods, a concentration of cultural facilities and a series of public-private partnerships to fund what were once public urban spaces. The result of this has been the growth of privately owned, semi-public spaces, often around shopping malls or so-called public squares such as Canary Wharf in London. Members of the general public are allowed in such spaces, but only if they fulfil certain criteria and refrain from a host of normal-seeming activities such as cycling, rollerblading or even eating. Some categories of citizen, such as homeless people, drug users or (as the Occupy movement found out) protestors are explicitly not wanted.

As the economic development of a city's culture has become more central, one particular type of urban policy coalition, the creative network, has become popular. In part this development was influenced by understandings of the role of intermediary institutions in industries such as textiles, but added to this was an understanding that, despite its role in international networks of capital and ideas, the cultural sector is very much rooted in particular places. Detailed knowledge of the local cultural scene is therefore important. Traditional arts agencies, used to offering grants to arts institutions within the networks of public subsidy, did not always have sufficient understanding of small cultural businesses, most of which (whether in new media, popular music, comedy or magazine production) did not see themselves as being in 'the arts'. This was not because their aims were purely commercial; it might be because their own identity, or the cultural form in which they work, such as a comedy club, was not seen as part of the subsidised arts sector.

Thus, many cities and regions have developed specialist policy agencies whose aim is to act as intermediaries between a heterogeneous and often ill-organised small-scale cultural sector and local or regional (and in some cases national or international) government. These agencies, sometimes established within local government and sometimes as an external agency, have to operate across private, public and voluntary cultural sectors and across policy areas such as planning and land use, as well as carry out the more specific task of helping cultural businesses with business information, advice and guidance.

As O'Connor and Gu (2013) have written in their account of one such agency, Manchester's Creative Industries Development service (CIDS), a crucial part of this intermediation was 'translating' not only the business needs but also the social, cultural and urbanistic concerns of cultural organisations into the language of economic development. Questions such as licensing laws (which govern bars and nightclubs), planning decisions, and policing or drugs policy were of interest to city centre cultural businesses. They were often concerned about maintaining a mixed economy of for-profit and voluntary organisations and were tolerant of different users of the urban realm, such as homeless people, drug users or sex workers. Traditional business support agencies were unlikely to reflect any of these concerns in their dealings with government, or at least not in the way that small cultural business may want them to be reflected.

Yet 'economic development', in the narrower sense of growth in businesses, jobs and turnover, was exactly what the many specialist agencies set up in the UK and elsewhere were generally tasked with promoting. These agencies were measured by the number of business they helped establish, the growth in jobs, the number of training places offered, and so on. While many of those who worked in such agencies tried hard to gain the trust of small cultural organisations, such trust was often undermined by the requirement to *measure* the effectives of such interactions. O'Connor and Gu's work suggests that CIDS in Manchester had aimed to traverse the ground between economic policy, urban planning and cultural policy, but that the requirements of funding, and indeed the way cultural policy is organised at national level – separating economic development from culture – meant that these splits were too deep. The organisation effectively closed in 2008, as policy in that part of northwest England became more concerned with the larger scale development of the BBC's 'Mediacity' (a relocation of parts of the national broadcaster to Salford). O'Connor and Gu's account reminds us of the difficulty of working across policy areas and with a multiplicity of agencies, but also of its necessity in the context of urban cultural policy.

CULTURE AND CONFLICT IN THE CITY

As this chapter makes clear, the city has become not only the prime site of cultural policy development in recent years but also a major site for its contestation. The need for cultural policy to engage with a range of urban policy issues and understand cultural production and consumption within the context of a place means that it consistently touches on broader political issues of public space, labour, community and identity. This is of course true of cultural policy at the national and global level as well, but the 'visibility' of cultural policy within a city – the new museum or the threatened skateboard park, the change in people's own neighbourhoods – brings these issues home to citizens in a way that disputes over copyright or cultural nationalism would struggle to do.

For many urban theorists, the city, while far from Utopia, remains the prime location for political activity, for resistance and for imagining of new political possibilities (e.g. Graeber 2013; Harvey [1989a] 2000, 2013; Pinder 2005). Well-known examples include organisations like Creative Class Struggle, a group of activists who not only take their name from Florida's work but are based in his current home town of Toronto. From here they write about activities, sometimes artist-led or involving artists, to oppose what they see as the gentrification, segregation and displacement that often follow from creative city urban strategies. Other examples have been the occupation of buildings in Hamburg by artists in an attempt to prevent them being sold to property developers, or squatters and artists joining forces in Berlin-Kreuzberg (Bader and Bialluch 2009), while in both Amsterdam and Barcelona artists have been at the forefront of attempts to resist gentrification of inner-city neighbourhoods (van de Geyn and Draaisma, 2009). In particular the plans of city authorities to impose new 'cultural quarters', often displacing existing artistic subcultures as well as low-income communities, has often been opposed by groups of cultural workers, not least as the rise in rent often associated with such developments tends to favour certain kinds of creative activity over others.

In recent years, what has become known as the Occupy movement (though it is probably best understood as a collection of movements rather than a single one) has sought to draw attention to glaring social and economic inequalities by establishing itself in temporary camps, often in significant urban locations, such as Wall Street in New York, Taksim Square in Istanbul and many more places. Not only does such activity make use of a cultural politics of protest – adopting the tropes of carnival to address sharp political questions – but, as David Harvey argues (2013), they bring together the concerns of young cultural workers, about pay, precarious work and unemployment, with related concerns about the costs of housing and education. While Harvey argues that 'pacification and professionalization' of the cultural workforce have blunted its once radical edges, he sees enough potential in its subcultures and growing discontent to believe it still makes fertile ground for leftist politics (Harvey 2013: 88). In doing so he appeals to a timeless notion of culture as 'something so special' that it can both absorb and resist commodification. Other forms of urban activism, from subtervising to guerrilla gardening, remind us of the oppositional role of cultural production and consumption in cities and the role of culture in both proffering critique and suggesting alternatives.

CONCLUSIONS

This chapter has argued that cities are where cultural policies become 'visible'. Historically, they have formed the space for cultural endowments, whether the result of patronage or faith, and while the national state might seem like the natural home for cultural policy and its analysis (see Chapter 5), nation-states often act out their cultural policies in the city, particularly (but not only) in capital cities. The dense networks of producers and consumers, markets and audiences that characterise cities lead to a concentration of cultural activities within them, and urban cultural policy seeks to take advantage of these factors to develop initiatives that are sometimes distinct from those of the national state.

Perhaps nowhere are geopolitical shifts more strongly reflected than in cities; in terms of size, the world's most important cities are located in the Global South, this will soon be reflected in economic terms, with twenty of the world's richest cities likely to be in Asia by 2025 (Mayor of London 2013). In recent years cities have increasingly been taking on responsibility for cultural policies; the ideas that animated the creative economy discourse were largely developed within cities in the Global North and, while many cities in the Global South have adopted these approaches, others are developing new ones, aiming for greater equity or stronger community involvement. The city's role as a laboratory for innovative cultural policy looks set to continue.

NOTES

1 See   http://www.unesco.org/new/en/culture/themes/creativity/creative-cities-network/
2 http://www.creativecity.ca/

REFERENCES AND FURTHER READING

Bader, I. and Bialluch, M. (2009) 'Gentrification and the creative class in Berlin Kreuzberg', in L.Porter and K.Shaw (eds) *Whose Urban Renaissance? An International Comparison of Urban Regeneration Strategies,* London: Routledge.

Bamford, A. (2006) *The Wow Factor: Global Research Compendium on the Impact of the Arts in Education,* Berlin: Waxmann Publishing.

Barnes, K., Waitt., G., Gill, N. and Gibson, C. (2006) 'Community and nostalgia in urban revitalisation: a critique of urban village and creative class strategies as remedies for social "problems"', *Australian Geographer* 37(3): 335–54.

Bell, D. (2014) 'Cottage economy: the "ruralness" of rural cultural industries', in K. Oakley and J. O'Connor (eds) *The Routledge Companion to the Cultural Industries,* London: Routledge.

Bell, D. and Jayne, M. (eds) (2004) *City of Quarters: Urban Villages in the Contemporary City,* Aldershot: Ashgate.

Bell, D. and Jayne, M. (2010) 'The creative countryside: policy and practice in the UK rural cultural economy', *Journal of Rural Studies*, 26(3): 209–18.

Bennett, T. (1992) 'Putting policy into cultural studies', in L. Grosberg, C. Nelson and P. Treichler (eds) *Cultural Studies*, London: Routledge.

Berry, M. (2005) 'Melbourne – is there life after Florida?', *Urban Policy and Research*, 23(4): 381–92.

Bianchini, F. (1987) 'GLC R I P, 1981–1986', *New Formations*, 1: 103–17.

——(1993) 'Remaking European cities: the role of cultural policies' in F. Bianchini and M. Parkinson (eds) *Cultural Policy and Urban Regeneration: the West European Experience*, Manchester: Manchester University Press.

BOP (2012) *World Cities Culture Report*, London: Mayor of London.

Bourdeau, J.-P. (2002) *Bowling Alone: Cross-indicators of Social Participation and Local Community Belonging in Canada*, Ottawa, ON: Strategic Research and Analysis Directorate, Department of Canadian Heritage.

Boyle, M. (2006) 'Culture in the rise of tiger economies: Scottish expatriates in Dublin and the "creative class" thesis', *International Journal of Urban and Regional Research*, 30(2): 403–26.

Brenner, N. and Theodore, N. (2002) 'Preface to special issue: from the new localism to the spaces of neoliberalism', *Antipode*, 34(3): 341–8.

Buck, N., Gordon, I., Harding, A. and Turok, I. (2005) *Changing Cities: Rethinking Urban Competitiveness, Cohesion and Governance*, Basingstoke: Palgrave MacMillan.

Cairncross, F. (1997) *The Death of Distance*, Cambridge MA: Harvard Business School Press.

Cameron, S. and Coafee, J. (2005) 'Art, gentrification and regeneration: from artist to pioneer to public arts', *European Journal of Housing Policy*, 5(1): 39–58.

CASE. (2010) *Understanding the drivers, impact and value of engagement in culture and sport*, London: Department for Culture, Media and Sport.

Coyle, D. (1997) *The Weightless World*, Cambridge MA: MIT Press.

Crewe, L. and Beaverstock, J. (1998) 'Fashioning the city: cultures of consumption in contemporary urban space's', *Geoforum*, 29(3): 287–308.

Currid, E. (2007) *The Warhol Economy: How Fashion, Art, and Music Drive New York City*, Princeton NJ: Princeton University Press.

Elsheshtawy, Y. (2012) 'The production of culture: Abu Dhabi's urban strategies', in *Cultural Policy and Governance in a New Metropolitan Age*, vol. 5, Cultures and Globalization, London: Sage.

Evans, G. (2001) *Cultural Planning: an Urban Renaissance?* Routledge: London.

——(2004) 'Cultural industry quarters: from pre-industrial to post-industrial production', in D. Bell and M. Jayne (eds) *City of Quarters: Urban Villages in the Contemporary City*, Aldershot: Ashgate.

Evans, G. and Shaw, P. (2004) *The Contribution of Culture to Regeneration in the UK: a Review of the Evidence*, London: DCMS.

Fanshawe, S. and Sriskandarajah, D. (2010) *You Can't Put me in a Box: Super-diversity and the End of Identity Politics*, London: Institute for Public Policy Research.

Florida, R. (2002) *The Rise of the Creative Class, and How it's Transforming Work, Leisure, Community and Everyday Life*, New York: Basic Books.

Florida, R. (2013) *More Losers than Winners in America's New Economic Geography*. Available at www.theatlanticcities.com/jobs-and-economy/2013/01/more-losers-winners-americas-new-economic-geography/4465/ (accessed 29/11/13).

Florida, R. and Tinagli, I. (2004) *Europe in the Creative Age*, London: Demos.

García, B. (2004) 'Urban regeneration, arts programming and major events', *International Journal of Cultural Policy*, 10(1): 103–18.

Gibson, C. (2013) 'Widening development pathways', paper absorbed into UNESCO, *The Creative Economy Report: Widening Local Development Pathways*, New York: UNESCO.

Gibson, C. and Klocker, N. (2005) 'The "Cultural Turn" in Australian regional economic development discourse: neoliberalising creativity?' *Geographical Research*, 43(1): 93–102.

Gilmore, A. (2013) 'Cold spots, crap towns and cultural deserts: The role of place and geography in cultural participation and creative place-making', *International Journal of Cultural Policy*, 22(2): 86–96.

GLA (2010) *London's Creative Workforce, 2009 Update*, Working Paper 40, London: GLA Economics.

Gonzalez, S. (2011) 'Bilbao and Barcelona "in motion": how urban regeneration "models" travel and mutate in the global flows of policy tourism', *Urban Studies*, 48(7): 1397–418.

Graeber, D. (2013) *The Democracy Project: a History, a Crisis, a Movement*, London: Allen Lane.

Grodach, C. and Silver, D. (eds) (2013) *The Politics of Urban Cultural Policy: Global Perspectives*, London: Routledge.

Hajer, M. and Reijndorp, A. (2001) *In Search of a New Public Domain*, Rotterdam: NAI Publishers.

Hall, P. (1998) *Cities and Civilisation: Culture, Technology and Urban Order*, London: Weidenfield and Nicolson.

Hannigan, J. (1998) *Fantasy City: Pleasure and Profit in the Postmodern Metropolis*, London: Routledge.

Harvey, D. (1989a) 'From managerialism to entrepreneurialism: the transformation of urban governance in late capitalism', *Geografiska Annaler*, 71(2): 3–17; reprinted in D. Harvey (2000) *Spaces of Hope*, Edinburgh: Edinburgh University Press.

——(1989b) *The Urban Experience*, Oxford: Oxford University Press.

——(2013) *Rebel Cities: From the Right to the City to the Urban Revolution*, London: Verso.

Harvey, D., Hawkins, H. and Thomas, N. (2012) 'Thinking creative clusters beyond the city: people, places and networks', *Geoforum*, 43: 529–39

Hui, D., Ng, C.-H. and Mok, P. (2004) *A Study on Hong Kong Creativity Index, Interim Report*, University of Hong Kong: Centre for Cultural Policy Research.

Jacobs, J. (1961) *The Death and Life of Great American Cities*, New York: Random House.

Jeannotte, M. (2003a) 'Singing alone? The contribution of cultural capital to social cohesion and sustainable communities', *International Journal of Cultural Policy*, 9(1): 35–49.

———(2003b) 'Just showing up: social and cultural capital in everyday life', in C. Andrew, M. Gattinger, M. Jeannotte, and W. Straw (eds) *Accounting for Culture: Thinking through Cultural Citizenship*, Ottawa, ON: University of Ottawa Press.

Kong, L. (2012) 'Ambitions of a global city: arts, culture and creative economy in "post-crisis" Singapore', *International Journal of Cultural Policy*, 18(3): 279–94.

Kong, L., Gibson, C, Khoo, L. and Semple, A. (2006) 'Knowledges of the creative economy: towards a relational geography of diffusion and adaptation in Asia', *Asia Pacific Viewpoint*, 47(2): 173–94.

Kong, L. and O'Connor, J. (eds) (2009) *Creative Economies, Creative Cities: Asian-European Perspectives*, Berlin: Springer Verlag.

Kunnemann, V. and Mayer, R. (eds) (2013) *Chinatowns in a Transnational World: Myths and Realities of an Urban Phenomenon*, London: Routledge.

Landry, C. (2000) *The Creative City: A Toolkit for Urban Innovators*, London: Earthscan.

Landry, C. and Bianchini, F. (1995) *The Creative City*, London: Demos.

LDA (2002) *Creativity: London's Core Business*, London: LDA.

———(2003) *Creative London*, London: LDA.

Lloyd, R. (2006) *Neo-bohemia: Arts and Commerce in the Post-industrial City*, New York: Routledge.

Luckman, S. (2012) *Locating Cultural Work: the Politics and Poetics of Rural, Regional and Remote Creativity*, Basingstoke: Palgrave Macmillan.

MacLennan, D. and Norman, B. (2004) *Glasgow and Melbourne: Remaking Two Great Victorian Cities*, presented at Resurgent Cities Conference, London School of Economics, 19–21 April.

Mayor of London (2013) *World Cities Culture Report*. London: Mayor of London.

McGranahan, D. and Wojan, T. (2007) 'Recasting the creative class to examine growth processes in rural and urban counties', *Regional Studies*, 41(2): 197–216.

Markusen, A. (2005) *Urban Development and the Politics of a Creative Class: Evidence from the Study of Artists*, presented at Regional Studies Association Conference on Regional Growth Agendas, Aalborg.

Markusen, A. and Gadwa, A. (2010a) 'Arts and culture in urban or regional planning', in N. Verma (ed.) *Institutions and planning*, Oxford: Elsevier.

Markusen, A. and Gadwa, A. (2010b) *Creative Placemaking. a White Paper for the Mayors' Institute on City Design*, Washington DC: National Endowment for the Arts.

Marshall, A. (1925) *Principles of Economics*, London: Macmillan.

Massey, D. (1994) *Space, Place and Gender*, Cambridge: Polity Press.

———(2007) *World City*, Cambridge: Polity Press.

Mercer, C. (2002) *Towards Cultural Citizenship: Tools for Cultural Policy and Development*, Hedemora: The Bank of Sweden Tercentenary Foundation and Gidlunds Forlag.

Moloch, H. (1976) 'The city as a growth machine', *American Journal of Sociology*, 82(2): 309–32.

Nichols Clark, T. and Silver, D. 2013. 'Chicago from the Political Machine to the Entertainment Machine' in C. Grodach and D. Silver (eds) *The Politics of Urban Cultural Policy: Global Perspectives*, London: Routledge

Oakley, K. (2009) 'Getting out of place: the mobile creative class takes on the local. A UK perspective on the creative class', in L. Kong and J. O'Connor (eds) *Creative Economies, Creative Cities: Asian-European Perspectives*, Berlin: Springer Verlag.

——(2012) 'Rich but divided ... the politics of cultural policy in London', in *Cultural Policy and Governance in a New Metropolitan Age*, vol. 5, Cultures and Globalization, London: Sage.

——(2013) 'A different class: politics and culture in London', in C. Grodach and D. Silver (eds) *The Politics of Urban Cultural Policy: Global Perspectives*, London: Routledge.

Oakley, K. and Pratt, A. (2010) *Brick Lane: Community-driven Innovation? Local Knowledge*, London: NESTA.

O'Connor, J. (2004) '"A special kind of city knowledge": innovative clusters, tacit knowledge and the "Creative City"', *Media International Australia*, 112: 131–49.

——(2006) 'Art, popular culture and cultural policy: variations on a theme of John Carey', *Critical Quarterly*, 48(4): 49–105.

——(2007) *The Cultural and Creative Industries: a Review of the Literature*, London: Creative Partnerships.

——(2009) 'Creative industries: a new direction?' *International Journal of Cultural Policy*, 15 (4): 387–402.

O'Connor, J. and Gu, X. (2013) 'Developing a creative cluster in a post-industrial city: CIDS and Manchester', in T. Flew (ed.) *Creative Industries and Urban Development: Creative Cities in the 21st Century*, London: Routledge.

ODPM (2004) *Our Cities are Back: Third Report of the Core Cities Working Group*, London: ODPM.

Pasotti, E. (2013) 'Brecht in Bogotá: how cultural policy transformed a clientelist political culture', in C. Grodach and D. Silver (eds) *The Politics of Urban Cultural Policy: Global Perspectives*, London: Routledge.

Peck, J. (2004) 'Geography and public policy: constructions of neoliberalism', *Progress in Human Geography*, 28(3): 392–405.

——(2005) 'Struggling with the creative class', *International Journal of Urban and Regional Research*, 20(4): 740–70.

Peck, J., Theodore, N. and Brenner, N. (2009) 'Neoliberal urbanism: models, moments, mutations', *SAIS Review*, 1: 49–66.

Peterson, R. and Kern, R. (1996) 'Changing highbrow taste: from snob to omnivore', *American Sociological Review*, 61(5): 900–7.

Pinder, D. (2005) *Visions of the City: Utopianism, Power and Politics in Twentieth-Century Urbanism*, Edinburgh: Edinburgh University Press.

Polanyi, M. (1966) *The Tacit Dimension*, Chicago: University of Chicago Press.

Polese, M. and Stren, R. (2000) *The Social Sustainability of Cities: Diversity and the Management of Change*, Toronto: University of Toronto Press.

Ponzini, D. (2013) 'Branded megaprojects and fading urban structure in contemporary cities', in G. del Cerro Santamaría (ed.) *Urban Megaprojects: a Worldwide View*, Bingley: Emerald.

Porter, M. (1998) 'Clusters and the new economics of competition', *Harvard Business Review*, 76(6): 77-90.

Pratt, A. (2000) 'New media, the new economy and new spaces', *Geoforum*, 31: 425–436.

——(2002) 'Hot jobs in cool places: the material cultures of new media product spaces: the case of the south of market, San Francisco', *Information, Communication and Society*, 5(1): 27–50.

——(2004) 'Creative clusters: towards the governance of the creative industries production system?' *Media International Australia*, 112: 50–66.

——(2005) 'Cultural industries and public policy: an oxymoron?' *International Journal of Cultural Policy*, 11(1): 31–44.

——(2006) 'Advertising and creativity, a governance approach: a case study of creative agencies in London', *Environment and Planning A*, 38: 1883–99.

——(2009) 'Urban regeneration: from the arts "feel good" factor to the cultural economy: A case study of Hoxton, London', *Urban Studies*, 46(5/6): 1041–61.

——(2011) 'Microclustering of the media industries in London', in R. Picard and C. Karlsson (eds) *Media Clusters*, Cheltenham: Edward Elgar.

——(2012). 'A world turned upside down: the creative economy, cities and the new austerity' in *Smart, Creative, Sustainable, Inclusive: Territorial Development Strategies in the Age of Austerity* London: Regional Studies Association.

Putnam, R. (2000) *Bowling Alone: The Collapse and Revival of American Community*, New York: Simon and Schuster.

Rausch, S. and Negrey, C. (2006) 'Does the creative engine run? A consideration of the effect of creative class on economic strength and growth', *Journal of Urban Affairs*, 28(5): 473–89.

Roche, M. (1998) 'Mega-events, culture and modernity: Expos and the origins of public culture', *International Journal of Cultural Policy*, 5(1): 1–31.

Romer, R. (1994) 'The origins of endogenous growth', *Journal of Economic Perspectives*, 8(1): 3–22.

Royseng, S. (2008) 'The ritual logic of cultural policy', paper presented at the Fifth International Conference on Cultural Policy Research, Istanbul, 20–24 August. Available from www2.warwick.ac.uk (accessed 01/12/13).

Sassen, S. (2001) *The Global City: New York, London, Tokyo*, Princeton NJ: Princeton University Press.

——(2006) *Cities in a World Economy*, third edition, Thousand Oaks CA: Pine Forge Press.

Scott A. (2000) *The Cultural Economy of Cities: Essays on the Geography of Image-producing Industries*, London: Sage.

——(2005) *On Hollywood: the place, the industry*, Princeton NJ: Princeton University Press.

——(2006) 'Creative cities: conceptual issues and policy questions', *Journal of Urban Affairs*, 28(1): 1–17.

Scott, A. and Power, D. (2004) *Cultural Industries and the Production of Culture*, New York: Routledge.

Silver, D. (2013) 'Local politics in the creative city: the case of Toronto', in C. Grodach and D. Silver (eds) *The Politics of Urban Cultural Policy: Global Perspectives*, London: Routledge.

Smith, N. (2003) 'New globalism, new urbanism: Gentrification as global urban strategy', in N. Brenner and N. Theodore (eds) *Spaces of Neoliberalism: Urban Restructuring in North America and Western Europe*, Oxford: Blackwell.

Stern M. and Seifert, S. (2000) *Cultural Participation and Communities: the Role of Individual and Neighborhood Effects*, Working Paper #13, SIAP: University of Pennsylvania.

——(2010) 'Cultural cluster: the implications of cultural assets agglomeration for neighbourhood revitalization', *Journal of Planning Education and Research*, 29(3): 262–79.

Stolarick, K. and Currid-Halkett, E. (2013) 'Creativity and the crisis: the impact of creative workers on regional unemployment', *Cities*, 33: 5–14.

Stolarick, K. and Florida, R. (2006) 'Creativity, connections and innovation: a study of linkages in the Montreal region', *Environment and Planning A*, 38: 1799–817.

Stolle, D. and Rochon, T. (1998) 'Are all associations alike? Member diversity, associational type and the creation of social capital', *American Behavorial Scientist*, 42(1): 47–65.

Sudjic, D. (1993) *The 100 Mile City*, London: Harcourt Publishers.

Thomas, N., Harvey, D. and Hawkins, H. (2013) 'Crafting the region: creative industries and practices of regional space', *Regional Studies*, 47: 75–88.

United Nations (2011) *World Population Prospects: The 2010 Revision*. New York: United Nations.

UNESCO (2013) *The Creative Economy Report: Widening Local Development Pathways*. New York: UNESCO.

van de Geyn, B. and Draaisma, J. (2009) 'The embrace of Amsterdam's creative breeding ground', in L. Porter and K. Shaw (eds) *Whose Urban Renaissance? an International Comparison of Urban Regeneration Strategies*, London: Routledge.

Waitt, G. (2004) 'Pyrmont-Ultimo: the newest chic quarter of Sydney', in D. Bell and M. Jayne (eds) *City of Quarters: Urban Villages in the Contemporary City*, Aldershot: Ashgate.

Waitt, G. and Gibson, C. (2009) 'Creative small cities: rethinking the creative economy in place', *Urban Studies*, 46(5/6): 1223–46.

Wood, P. and Landry, C. (2008) *The Intercultural City: Planning for Diversity Advantage*, London: Earthscan.

Yeoh, B. (2005) 'The global cultural city? Spatial imagineering and politics in the (multi)cultural marketplaces of South-east Asia', *Urban Studies*, 42(5/6): 945–58.

Yudice, G. (2009) 'Culture-based urban development in Rio de Janeiro', in R. Biron (ed.) *CITY/ART: the Urban Scene in Latin America*, Durham NC: Duke University Press.

Zukin, S. (1982) *Loft Living: Culture and Capital in Urban Change*, Baltimore: Johns Hopkins University Press.

——(1995) *The Culture of Cities*, Oxford: Blackwell.

5

NATIONAL CULTURAL POLICY

Two news items from the summer of 2013 provide us with an entry point for our discussion of cultural policy and the nation. The first concerns an idea floated by the French president, Francois Hollande, to apply a tax to smartphones, tablets and laptops. The revenue thus collected would be used to support French cultural production – music, art and film (Willsher 2013). After nine months of deliberation, a 'special culture committee' made this proposal, along with 75 others, in a move to protect France's 'cultural exception' (see Chapter 6). The second story, appearing on a British national newspaper's blog, focusses on the UK's culture minister, Maria Miller. It reports doubts about her capability in the role, wondering whether she might be the last UK minister for culture – might even preside over the disbanding of the Department for Media, Culture and Sport (DCMS), a ministry established (or at least rebranded) by the incoming Labour government in 1997. Doubts about Miller and about the DCMS are cast in the shadow of austerity and cuts in government funding – and the arts are often a soft target for such cuts (Higgins 2013).

So, on the one hand we have a story about protection and exception, on the other about the vulnerability of state support for culture and doubts over the very purpose of a government department for culture. Stories like this repeat through the history of national cultural policy: what is the right role for the state in matters of art and culture? How should the state intervene? And is the infrastructure of the state an appropriate mechanism for 'managing' culture, by either protection or promotion? In this chapter we trace the playing out of such questions through a focus on the scale of the nation. The nation might seem like the 'natural home' for cultural policy and its analysis, but as we shall see, there is considerable contest over the national state's role in culture, and even more variation in how that role plays out. Our discussion also considers ways of studying national cultural policy, examining single-nation 'case studies' as well as comparative research. We begin with one of the best known, but also most controversial, aspects of national cultural policy: uses of culture in the service of celebrating the nation.

GRAND NATIONAL

In less than two decades, the UK has been the stage for two immense, expensive stagings of national culture: the celebrations of the turning of the new millennium, which here were centred on the Millennium Dome, and the hosting of the London 2012 Olympic Games. Both events aimed at a global audience as much as a national one, and both aimed to conjure positive images of Britain as (at the very least) a competent organiser of big parties and (at the most) as a major global player in the field of culture. Hosting so-called mega-events is a well-used strategy in cultural policy, and one with a long history (Roche 2000). There is a particular lineage connecting the Great Exhibition of the Works of Industry of All Nations in 1851, the 1951 Festival of Britain, and the New Millennium Experience – even if, in reality, the context and motive for each event were very different (McGuigan 2004). To borrow from subtitles of studies of the earlier two mega-events, the Great Exhibition was 'a nation on display' (Auerbach 1999), while the Festival of Britain presented 'the autobiography of a nation' (Conekin 2003). Both, however, parlayed the national and the international side by side, set in an imperial context (but, of course, that context meant very different things in

1951 than it did a century earlier). By the time we fast-forward to the 1999/2000 turning of the millennium we have an even more different global and national context – though the rhetoric around the Dome has clear echoes of the history of mega-eventing Britain. Here's the then prime minister, Tony Blair, laying out his ambition for the Dome:

> This is Britain's opportunity to greet the world with a celebration that is so bold, so beautiful, so inspiring that it embodies at once the spirit of confidence and adventure in Britain and the spirit of the future of the world.
>
> (Blair 1998, quoted in McGuigan 2004: 77)

In the same speech, Blair explicitly connected back to 1951 and 1851, tracing a line of very British exceptionalism: a rebuttal to critics of the Dome which uses history to argue that such criticism is false, and at the same time a restatement of Britain's standing on the world stage.

Jim McGuigan (2004) connects projects like the Dome to one of the three 'improper' uses of culture by the state outlined in a famous comment by Raymond Williams (1984), already flagged in Chapter 2: Williams comments critically on the state's tendency to harness culture in the service of 'national aggrandizement' – a form of 'display' of national cultural might and prowess. Mega-events – including, in the UK, those associated with royalty (coronations and assorted royal weddings, christenings and funerals) – are a key form of national cultural display, running alongside the hosting of various travelling shows such as the Olympics, as well as the countless forms of investment in and promotion of culture in the service of national publicity, whether internally focussed (reminding ourselves how great we are) or externally targeted (reminding the world how great we are). And while national aggrandisement is itself a worldwide cultural phenomenon – no nation is likely to undersell its cultural accomplishments – in the story of national cultural policy, some nations are seen as more aggressively self-aggrandising than others. In this type of account, France is often singled out as the self-publicist *par excellence*, especially in the so-called *grands projets* associated with the presidency of Francois Mitterand and his culture minister Jack Lang (Looseley 1995). The strategy of the *grands projets* involved the building of major cultural institutions – often called flagships – with a strong emphasis on their architectural greatness. Among the *projets* of this period are the renovated and remodelled Louvre, the Opera Bastille and the Bibliotheque Nationale. As David Looseley (1995: 139) summarises, a key aim of these new (or renewed) cultural institutions was 'to reassert but redefine a national culture' – to build new monuments to France's exceptional culture (or cultural exception). As with the tax on smartphones that we started this chapter with, we see here the twinning of that notion of exception – that French culture is special – with the need for protection, or at least the sense that state intervention is needed to hold back some form of loss of or threat to that very cultural exception (the economic notion of 'cultural exception' – that cultural goods are 'special' and should be treated differently than other goods; see also Chapter 6). Looseley writes that in part, Mitterand and Lang's ambition was to 'energise French society itself, *restoring* France's self-confidence' (140; our emphasis). As we shall see later, this particular twinning hangs over much state cultural policy. Moreover, the notion of the need for the state to intervene to shore up national identity recurs throughout our analysis of the national scale. In fact, we might argue that at the heart of national cultural policy is a particular form of instrumentalism: the use of culture to create, and continually reiterate, national identity.

IMAGINED COMMUNITIES, INVENTED TRADITIONS, BANAL NATIONALISMS

> The nation state created an entirely new and unprecedented institution of culture and cultural policy. In the nation-state era, cultural policy has essentially been about shaping and managing national cultural orders. The central objective has been to create a sense of belonging and allegiance to the national community
>
> (Robins 2007: 150)

There is an obvious connection between culture and nation formation, therefore: culture is conscripted into helping define the nation. Exploring the histories of nation-building and national identity, commentators have often singled out various forms of culture as a kind of glue that binds a nation, that defines its 'nation-ness'. A key concept here is the nation as an imagined community (Anderson 1991), and the steering of the imaginative work of making a nation cohere and self-identify is often down to culture. Historians remind us that nations are 'fictions', so it should come as no surprise to see cultural production and consumption centrally implicated in the storying of the nation, providing the core narratives around which national identity can coalesce (DeVereaux and Griffin 2013; Minnaert 2014). Given culture's role in providing imaginative resources and in facilitating forms of 'identity-work', we can see how forms of culture-as-display might work to bond members of an imagined nation together – furnishing, as Robins (2007: 150) puts it, 'the national *imaginaire*'. The mega-events highlighted above are certainly part of this arsenal: in the UK, conventional (though contested) wisdom highlights the coronation of Queen Elizabeth II in 1953 as a key modern moment of national bonding, facilitated by a then newly emerging cultural technology: television (McGuigan 2004).

The communal gathering around the TV set at times of high national importance, whether royal, sporting or some other kind, can be slotted into a second useful way of understanding culture's national project: the notion of invented tradition (Hobsbawn and Ranger 1983). Here, we see how part of nation-building through culture uses rediscoveries or inventions of national pasts in the service of present and future nation-building. Over time, the 'inventedness' of these traditions pales and they become part of the ordinary cultural life of the nation, ticking along in the background. In many modern societies, television has become a central place for new traditions to be invented, especially where there are national-coverage state TV stations, such as the BBC in the UK. Live TV enables the simultaneous experiencing of moments of national celebration, and therefore of the restoration of national self-confidence.

Of course, such moments are open to contestation and rejection – in recent years in the UK the invented tradition of the Queen's Christmas Day speech has been countered by 'alternatives' on other channels – but in their repetition they quietly perform important work, reminding us that we belong, willingly or not, to a particular nation (and, of course, reminding 'others' that they do not belong). Watching the national news on TV or reading a national newspaper every day reinforces a sense of 'nation-ness', despite ideological differences among national media providers. Ongoing debates about the role and value of the BBC as the 'nation's broadcaster' in the UK may make it appear as if the nation is fragmenting, at least around its everyday media practices, but the very fact of the debate itself becomes a kind of invented tradition, a collective reflection of what being British, and having a *British* Broadcasting Corporation, means today (O'Brien 2013). Moaning about BBC bias or the licence fee, or cherishing 'Auntie Beeb', is all part of a specifically national conversation.

Much of the work of community imagining and tradition inventing takes place in the realm of everyday life; while exceptional events might loom large as moments when the nation was reimagined – in the UK's recent past, the funeral of Princess Diana is often discussed in this context (McGuigan 2004) – much cultural nation-building is made up of small acts or forms of banal nationalism (Billig 1995). Taking an interest in various national sporting teams is perhaps the most obvious example. Even mega-projects and *grands projets* contain elements of banal nationalism, not least in their attempts to 'rebrand' the nation in the context of globalisation. And equally importantly, the national conversation around any proposed *grand projet*, including critical comment, similarly serves to restate what the nation's values are (McNeill and Tewdwr-Jones 2003). A flagship cultural institution quickly becomes part of the 'furniture', whether loved or loathed.

At other times and in other places, the state's role in orienting national identity via culture may be more hands-off; this is in itself a form of banal nationalism in that it reinforces the function of national political culture and therefore speaks to national identity: *we don't believe in government intervention in areas of national life like culture.* Cultural policy thus becomes a measure or marker of national character in a broader sense – the very doing of national cultural policy is a statement about culture and about the nation-state.

NATIONAL CHARACTER

> Underlying the legal and administrative surface of any state cultural policy, there exists a mix of historical trajectories, tactical choices, economic premises and the *unique cultural features* of its national target areas.
>
> (Häyrynen 2013: 623, our emphasis)

To understand national cultural policy, we need to understand the nation whose culture is being made a policy target. This seems straightforward, with no chicken-and-egg conundrums to resolve. In practice, unravelling cultural policy from national culture can be a complicated task. Yet in the study of national cultural policy, this is one dominant approach. Mark Schuster (2002) refers to this as the 'descriptive literature' in cultural policy studies: single-site 'case studies' that account for cultural policy formation in the context of national culture, national politics and national character. The Frenchness of French cultural policy – bold, centralised, borderline arrogant, anti-American – contrasts with the more modest (but still interventionist) character of British cultural policy, and the supposed disdain for national cultural policy (and government meddling in general) evident in the USA (though this idea of US cultural policy is itself contested, as we shall see later). As Kevin Mulcahy (2000: 138) puts it, in this stereotypical view 'the American government is often viewed as a reluctant patron of culture with a parsimonious and puritanical bent. In contrast, the conventional wisdom sees European national governments as longtime, generous and unstinting benefactors of culture'. As this statement shows, it is often with regard to approaches to cultural patronage that national character is described. This question is posed in an edited collection exploring just this theme: *Who's to Pay for the Arts?* (Cummings and Schuster 1989).

Discussing Anglo-French cultural (policy) difference, David Looseley (2011) notes another key aspect of national identity: the definition of an 'other' who is not like 'us'. As he writes, 'one notices how often UK arts circles have cast France as Britain's amusingly verbose "other", a foil that reassures Britons about the solid "common sense" of their thinking' (366). Yet at the same time, he notes, the UK arts sector sometimes looks enviously across the Channel, spying apparently lavish spending on French culture that lacks a UK equivalent. Now, Looseley quickly reminds us that these views merely trade on national stereotypes (on both sides of the water). Nevertheless, there is, in the 'descriptive literature', an attempt to explain national cultural policy by reflecting not only on political culture (see next section) but also to a looser notion of 'national character'. The alleged lack of nation-scale cultural policy in the USA, therefore, is attributed at least in part to a distaste for Big Government that is in itself part political egg, part cultural chicken. Whatever the truth of this alleged lack, its repetition in various discourses – including those of cultural policy studies – continues its own act of banal nationalism, reiterating something about US national character, US politics and US cultural policy, all at once.

One way in which the academic literature has approached this question is through the development of typologies – classificatory frameworks that enable researchers to sort and order national cultural policy. Perhaps the best known and most widely used classification is Chartrand and McCaughey's (1989) fourfold typology of arts patronage (see Table 5.1).

In this typology, then, the USA exemplifies a 'facilitator state' role, funding the arts via tax exemption or donation (often with match funding acting as a lever), the UK is a 'patron state' devolving cultural policy implementation to so-called arm's-length bodies;

Table 5.1 Models of national support for the arts

Role of the state	Model country	Policy objective	Funding system
Facilitator	USA	Diversity	Tax exemption
Patron	UK	Excellence	Arm's-length arts councils
Architect	France	Social welfare	Ministry of culture
·gineer	Soviet Union	Political education	Ownership of means of artistic production

·ased on Bordat 2013 (derived from Chartrand and McCaughey 1989) meanwhile the French 'architect state' uses state bureaucracy directly and aims to enhance social welfare via the arts, and the Soviet 'engineer state' directly controls artistic production. Now, as with any typology, this seemingly simple matrix hides a fair amount of overlap and ambiguity; as Bordat (2013) shows in her attempt to deploy this grid to Latin American states, and particularly Mexico, there is sometimes a rather awkward fit to be made. Moreover, the matrix is static and does not reflect change over time. Looseley (2011) comments that British and French models of cultural policy can be seen to converge in recent times – and to converge more towards the French approach, not least in terms of the balance of policy objective between access and excellence. Beyond this apparently neat (or neatened) fourfold classification, other 'models' of cultural policy have been described, such as the Nordic model – based around artistic freedom and cultural democracy, but also contested for its tidying up of a more complex regional picture (Dueland 2008; Mangset *et al.* 2008). Such caveats not-withstanding, the Nordic model has been sketched like this (based on Mangset *et al.* 2008):

- Welfare-oriented (in terms of the welfare role of the arts and welfare support for artists)
- Strong artists' organisations with strong links to public sector
- High levels of public subsidy and scepticism of market/private funding
- Egalitarian cultural life with stress on access
- Fairly high levels of cultural homogeneity
- Key role for cultural policy in national identity
- Expanded definition of 'culture' to include sectors such as sport
- Strong decentralisation to local and regional levels
- Mix of 'facilitator' and 'patron' model of national cultural policy administration – strong cultural ministries and strong arts councils

Peter Dueland (2008) offers a useful critical commentary on this model, highlighting differences between the Nordic countries and change over time. Notably, since the mid-2000s he sees a 'massive reawakening of the national dimension in official cultural policy' (18) – this leads him to surmise that national cultural policy can be read as a symbol (or symptom) of shifting ideologies of nationalism, with Nordic countries such as Denmark refocussing cultural policy onto the 'question of Danishness'. How such shifts will recast or reshape the Nordic model is a matter of ongoing investigation.

Also operating at a supranational/regional level, attempts have been made to classify European cultural policy. Rius Ulldemolins and Rubio Arostegui (2013) draw on this lineage of European typologies to propose yet another fourfold matrix, which folds in a variant the previously discussed Nordic model. This group comprises (i) the Continental-European model (France is once again the exemplar), (ii) the Scandinavian model (a renaming of the Nordic); (iii) the Anglo-Saxon model, and (iv) the Mediterranean model. However, in their subsequent discussion of Spain they see a more mixed picture (Madrid is more like type (i), Barcelona type (iii)). The trouble with typologies is made clear: while they offer us a neat set of boxes into which we can sort national cultural policy approaches, in reality it can be hard to find exactly the right box. One solution, of course, is to re-label the boxes until everything fits: Kevin Mulcahy keeps returning to this problem, reframing the typology and renaming the boxes. In a 2006 discussion he proposes a fourfold classification of 'cultural value-systems' comprising patrimony (France), identity (Quebec), social welfare (Nordic) and libertarian (USA); he had earlier devised a slightly different typology.

Table 5.2 Typology of public cultures and systems of cultural patronage

Mode of public culture	Representative nation	Cultural administration	Cultural funding model	Cultural politics
Nationalistic	France	Statist	Subsidy	Hegemony
Social-democratic	Norway	Localistic	Entitlement	Redistribution
Liberal	Canada	Consociational	Grant	Sovereignty
Libertarian	USA	Pluralist	Tax exemption	Privatisation

Source: based on Mulcahy 2000

Re-dividing, reclassifying and renaming gives us different ways of thinking about the similarities and distinctions between particular national cultural policy frameworks, for sure. But adding yet more choices of typology, shuffling the boxes, can also end in confusion. Despite an apparent fondness for fourfold grids, we might begin to question this apparent neatness. Can we really fit the world (of national cultural policy) into four boxes?

One solution is to simply add another box. 'New' models of national cultural policy are described and therefore new boxes created, often hybridising existing forms: in Japan, Nobuko Kawashima (2012: 296) identifies strong corporate involvement in cultural patronage leading to the birthing of

> an original model of cultural support, somewhere between the corporate philanthropy that is traditional in the USA and the arts sponsorship that is primarily commercial and prevalent in Europe where the public sector is the major player in cultural policy.

Again, the national character and culture of Japan helps explain this new model: corporate involvement in the arts is not framed in terms of commercial gain but in terms of promoting broader societal well-being – this well-being is seen as beneficial for business; it is thus a form of 'enlightened self-interest' (296) in line with a broader reorientation of Japanese corporate culture. And our list could go on. How many boxes will be enough in the end?

Of course, cultural policy's connection to national character isn't only about typologies and boxes. As we noted earlier, there is a broader sense of this connection: that the Danes will inevitably have their kind of cultural policy, just as the British or Japanese will. National identity is both produced by and producer of cultural policy, therefore. Sometimes, policy interventions might be attempts to redefine national character or address a national stereotype, at home or abroad. In this regard, Pertti Alasuutari (2001: 174) discusses debate around the problematic image of Finnish people in the 1980s and 1990s as 'uncivilized, rowdy lager louts', especially when they leave their home country. Here, cultural policy is seen as a way to intervene in this crisis, to 'correct' this external image of the Finnish nation via art and education policy. There was also,

Alasuutari writes, a perceived need to reorient Finland towards Europe, and part of this reorientation involved 'supporting art that complies with classical European standards' (175). Also wrestling with the issue of official national culture in the context of national character and reputation, Myrsini Zorba (2009) explores Greek cultural policy since the end of the Second World War. Here, a strong idea of national culture, based largely on heritage, is understood and utilised in different periods to suit different political objectives, as Greece is repositioned geopolitically, and as elite and popular culture are re-valued. As Zorba describes, the ancient history of Greece is both a blessing and a curse to the country; a redefinition of 'Greekness' must deal with that past even during periods of modernisation. In the policy field, then, Greekness must be negotiated – and so the Greekness of Greek cultural policy becomes a manifestation of that negotiation. One key element of this is, as noted already, the political culture in which cultural policy is developed. As Zorba's history tells us, Greek cultural policy in the post-war period was 'dependent on the specific political circumstances of the time' (256): policy and politics interact.

POLICY AND POLITICS

> To understand the cultural politics of a country, one must first understand its political culture.
>
> (Ridley 1987: 225)

The descriptive literature of single-site studies returns again and again to this interaction. Bordat (2013: 236) summarises the key question: 'does political change affect cultural policy?' Looking in particular at major 'regime change' in Mexico in the year 2000, her conclusion might come as a surprise: 'Mexican cultural policy followed a particular path that has not known important changes to its objectives and bureaucratic organization, in spite of the political alternation and regime change in 2000. ... Mexican cultural policy has barely changed' (241). Her summation is that policy change does not come easily. Why is this?

To understand why 'regime change' does or does not lead to cultural policy change we need to return to an understanding of the policy process and remember the key players in that process. In many cases, the actual authors and advocates of policy are bureaucrats rather than politicians, so political regime change may not necessarily affect their work. Of course, when a new government takes over, it may want to signal its radical new direction by culling existing policies and creating new ones. The culling can be politically important if pre-existing policies are too strongly associated with the previous government; even successful or popular policies are not immune if they are seen as too ideologically tainted. Dave O'Brien (2012) gives the example of the Free Swimming programme in the UK – part of New Labour's sports (and health) policy (and proposed Olympic legacy) that provided £140 million in funding to local authorities for the provision of free sessions in municipal pools for the under-16s and over-60s. The scheme was quickly discarded by the incoming Coalition government keen to find easy targets for spending cuts (and O'Brien argues that the economic argument was foregrounded, masking party political and ideological rationales).

Yet, as the Mexico example shows, often the opposite is true: a change of government does *not* lead to sudden or seismic policy change. As policy scholars have shown, by the time a policy is adopted and implemented, there is so much invested in it that culling is not that simple. Moreover, a policy can be effectively rebranded, stripped of its previous political colouring and claimed by the incoming administration. In a study of Finnish cultural policy from 1990 to 2010, Simo Häyrynen (2013: 626) reaches a similar conclusion: 'Although the variation in parliamentary power relations and the ideological background of the ministers of culture has been considerable, it has not changed the course of cultural policy'. And reviewing the UK case, Ken Worpole (2001: 245) concludes that 'the continuities of policy and practice in the past fifty years of national cultural policy have been far greater than any processes of development or change'. As he notes, the incoming Labour government of 1997 effectively inherited the planned millennium celebration from their Conservative predecessors, turning it into (for better or worse) an iconic 'New Labour' project. Similarly, the Coalition inherited the 2012 Olympics. Obviously, halting such juggernauts of cultural policy would be almost impossible, unlike cancelling the free swimming scheme, so perhaps the only option is often to try to disconnect party politics from cultural policy and carry on regardless. And while we might expect to be able to second-guess how a swing to the left or the right will reshape national cultural policy, empirical studies sometimes prove us wrong: Kate MacNeill and colleagues (2013) have looked into the correlation between arts funding and party-political ideology over a 40-year period in Australia, and actually found a surprising *lack* of correlation, despite, as they put it, 'a [presumed] association between Labor governments and government support for the arts', leading them to conclude that 'the particular character of the government itself is just as important as its party political persuasion' (MacNeill *et al*. 2013: 3, 15). Where they do find correlation is between government reviews and expenditure; so, a government that initiates a review of support for the arts is likely to increase its support as a result of the review.

Interestingly, the typologies described above do not account explicitly for party politics; they assume that regime change will not have a major impact on the character of national cultural policy: the USA will be a facilitator state whether a Republican or Democrat sits in the White House, though inevitably the detail will be party-politically coloured. Sometimes, of course, political change might lead to the need to move a particular country from one box to another: how 'French' does British cultural policy need to become before it's rebadged from patron to architect?

It seems, therefore, that the most we can say on this matter is that sometimes cultural policy changes when governments change, and sometimes not. Sometimes a policy is too closely associated with a particular administration to survive an election, but other policies live on, either because they are not seen as weighed down by ideological baggage or because they are amenable to having that baggage repacked by a new government. At times even apparently large party-political swings lead as much to continuity as change: in the UK, New Labour might have renamed the previous Department of National Heritage (DNH) as the DCMS, but beneath the surface, existing policies lived on. At the time of writing, the DCMS itself lives on, though as we noted at the start of this chapter there have been rumblings about its future.

A possible disbanding of the department would surely mark a lurch away from France, in terms of national character and culture, even though the jury is still out on how effective the DCMS has been to date (Gray and Wingfield 2011). In part this uncertainty surrounding the DCMS is connected to the ways arts and government are brought together (and kept apart) in the UK – through use of the so-called 'arm's-length principle'.

HOW LONG IS AN ARM'S LENGTH?

Part of the capacity for policies to survive, especially in the area of culture, might be accounted for, at least in cases like the UK, by the limited direct involvement of the government in the management of cultural affairs. Thanks to a clever invention called the arm's-length principle, the British government (and other fellow users) is able to distance itself from thorny decision-making, while the cultural sector is to some extent insulated from government meddling (allegedly, at least). Robert Hewison (1995) argues that while the term 'arm's-length principle' only appears in the cultural policy lexicon in the 1970s, its origins in Britain trace back to 1919 and the establishment of an unelected body called the University Grants Committee, charged with the allocation of higher education funding.[1] With the founding of the Arts Council of Great Britain (ACGB) in 1946, this principle was imported into arts policy, promising a degree of distance between politicians and artists.

Critics have repeatedly argued, however, that the arm's length is remarkably short in Britain – and Raymond Williams (1979) extends the corporeal analogy, noting that it is the body (government) that controls what the arm does. Williams also returns to the issue of national character in his critique, specifically the character of the British ruling class: the unelected members of the Arts Council were all representatives of the ruling elite, just like the politicians they were supposedly distant from. As such, Williams concluded, 'they will act as if they were indeed state officials' (quoted in Hewison 1995: 33). Also commenting on the relationship between the formation of the Arts Council, the arm's-length principle, and national character, albeit from a very different vantage point, its architect John Maynard Keynes remarked in 1945 on how 'English' the process had been: 'an important thing has happened. State patronage of the arts has crept in. It has happened in a very English, informal unostentatious way – half-baked, if you like' (quoted in Hewison 1995: 44). So, from its very beginning, the arm's-length Arts Council model is imbued with Englishness – and it continues to define the box into which UK cultural policy is placed to this day.

However, the relative merits and demerits of the arm's-length principle are continually debated, while the exact nature of the principle invites ongoing critique: in the era of the DNH, the principle was redescribed as 'arm's-length but hands on' (Gray 2000: 148), while one-time chairman of the Arts Council Sir Christopher Frayling sarcastically commented that by the mid-2000s the arm's length had shortened to 'Venus de Milo's length' (in Alexander 2008: 1424). Certainly, within the arts community there are doubts expressed about the real length of this arm (Gray 2008; Quinn 1997). And while the arts might be a 'special case' that politicians are especially allergic to, we need also to understand that the arm's-length principle reflects a broader history of the British state's view on appropriate levels and forms of intervention: the formation of ACGB needs to be read alongside the immediate post-war political climate and especially alongside the formation of the welfare state (Gray 2000; Hewison 1995). So the length of a British arm is distinctive; in other countries the issue of state involvement in culture has played out very differently – from the Soviet 'engineer' model to the US 'facilitator'. That said, even in such different contexts the length of an arm can change.

In the USA, for example, the federal government has generally been seen as hands-off in regard to the arts. In its facilitator role, the state has created space for private patronage and philanthropy, encouraged through tax incentives at most – an approach described by one commentator as 'uniquely American' (Netzer 1978: 13). Or so the mythology goes. In actual fact, there are examples of direct involvement in the arts by the US state, for instance the New Deal arts programmes of the 1930s and the formation of the National Endowment for the Arts (NEA) in 1965 – in fact, Miller and Yudice (2002: 37) argue that the USA 'actually invented modern cultural policy in a Federal frame', tracking it back to the late eighteenth century (see also Mulcahy 1987). And while they repeat a frequently quoted retort from President Nixon in the sixties – 'the arts are not our people' (48) – Miller and Yudice tell a more complex story of bodies like the NEA, including the story of its rise to notoriety in the late 1980s following claims that it was subsidising pornography. In its design, however, the NEA spun an American version of arm's length, similarly seeking to 'keep politics out' of the funding process through the creation of a labyrinthine bureaucratic structure (see Mulcahy 1987: 315). In the US case, of course, there is also considerable decentralisation in cultural policy (see below).

Measuring an arm's length offers another opportunity for typologies and sorting. Matarasso and Landry (1999) describe a continuum for assessing various so-called 'strategic dilemmas' in state cultural policy, one of which concerns distribution of state funding: should it be directly controlled by the state, or insulated from the political process? Adapting this continuum, Christopher Madden (2009) explicitly connects it to the arm's-length principle. Madden shows how key characteristics of the arm's-length principle can be mapped onto Matarasso and Landry's continuum, such as who is tasked with decision-making powers: at one end of the spectrum are 'ordinary citizens' and right at the other end are appointed ministers. Clearly, the more one moves from former to latter, the shorter the arm becomes. Madden also notes considerable conceptual confusion over the arm's-length principle, including confusion over its status as a *principle* and slippage between definitions based around (i) the presence of an autonomous funding body and (ii) peer assessment decision-making. Moreover, the 'principle' is seen as an ideal type rarely if ever achieved in practice (Quinn 1997), while reviews suggest convergence towards a mixed model of arts support, combining arts council and ministry approaches (Schuster 1985; Madden 2009). In countries like the UK this mixing involves shortening the arm's length, and is attributed at least in part to broader trends in policy, such as the rise of the 'new public management' and the 'instrumentalisation' of culture. As we shall see, this convergence narrative is repeated across comparative studies of national cultural policy formations.

So far, we have mainly considered the arm's-length principle in relation to arts funding. And this has certainly been a major focus of academic and policymaking attention. But, as the case of the NEA in the 1980s and 1990s shows, federal funding for culture cannot be fully divorced from other considerations – in that case, the issue of censorship. Regardless of the length of the arm, the state can be readily implicated in cultural controversy if there is a traceable line back to government. This opens up a bigger question, therefore: how should the state 'manage' cultural production and consumption?

PROHIBIT, PROTECT, PROMOTE

We can oversimplify the state's role vis-à-vis culture down to three possibilities: that its main functions are to (i) control, censor and prohibit forms of cultural expression, (ii) provide forms of protection for national culture, and (iii) promote national culture and enlist culture in broader national promotion. In practice, of course, these categories are not so neat. Nevertheless, we can begin here to map out some ways in which the state performs each of these three roles.

In terms of prohibition, the most obvious activity is state censorship: in the 'engineer' model of national cultural policy, the state directly owns and controls the means of cultural production and so can decide what counts as legitimate culture and what does not. In so-called 'command cultures' (Miller and Yudice 2002), the state has an interest in promoting authorised forms of culture while policing those deemed illegitimate – so even here prohibition runs side by side with promotion. Away from more obvious forms of censorship, subtle control of cultural production and consumption often takes place, for example through funnelling funds towards some types of culture and away from others (Alexander 2008): what we might think of as 'soft censorship'.

In terms of protection, we saw at the beginning of this chapter a recent example in the proposed French smartphone tax. The history of national cultural policy is littered with countless attempts – successful and otherwise – to protect national culture. This can take the form of preservation, as in heritage policies concerned with protecting the past from disappearing. It can be aimed at keeping at bay 'threatening' cultural forces from outside, threats variously framed as 'cultural imperialism', 'globalisation' or 'the market'. Here, a defensive nationalism might be evident, attempting to protect and preserve what is considered distinctive about national culture. A central problem with preservationist protectionism is its tendency to fix or freeze national culture, to turn the nation into a heritage museum. In a globalised era, the making of such a museum seems untenable by definition, and state attempts to define national culture prove increasingly fraught:

> national cultural policy objectives become intrinsically more difficult in a global context, in which local cultural expression becomes difficult to separate from the effects of Hollywood cinema, highstreet fashion, popular music, MTV and CNN. Cultural institutions seem less relevant when so much art and culture finds people by everyday routes.
>
> (Craik *et al.* 2003: 29)

Nevertheless, as in the French case, the discourse of the cultural exception continues to lend weight to forms of protectionism. In the UK too, sectors like film continue to try to mobilise forms of protection and – in this instance – define what constitutes a British film; recent attempts to create a 'culture test' that a film production must pass to be eligible for tax incentives show the difficulty and also the persistence of this form of cultural protectionism (Dickinson and Harvey 2005; Magor and Schlesinger 2009; Newsinger 2012).

The case of UK film policy produces an interesting hybridisation in that it sits (sometimes uneasily) at the intersection of trade policy and cultural policy: film is treated as industry and as art (Dickinson and Harvey 2005). So here protection meets promotion, in a different formulation – and one increasingly familiar in national cultural policy in the UK and elsewhere, as culture takes on a 'trade' or 'industrial' character, as in the dominant policy discourse of the creative industries and the turn towards the economic 'instrumentalisation' of culture. National studies from around the world show just how pervasive this turn has been: in South Korea, Kwon and Kim (2013) plot a move from state censorship to industrial development in cultural policy, while in Singapore, Lily Kong (2000) sees the state increasingly emphasising an economic agenda for culture (though this discourse is resisted by the arts community, which favoured a socio-cultural role for the arts and rejected the state's economism).

Like the convergence noted earlier, here we see the promotional use of culture gaining ground in different national contexts. Note that the 'promotional' aspect is twofold: the state takes on the role of cultural impresario, using trade/industry methods to 'sell' culture; at the same time, culture is used to promote or 'sell' the nation. The success of the so-called Korean Wave of popular culture tells both stories at once – a realisation of the economic value of the cultural industries combined with an understanding of the value of making Korean popular culture go global, embodied in the 'K-pop' star Psy's worldwide success with the song 'Gangnam Style' (Kwon and Kim 2013). While there is a particular story here, of Korean popular culture and Korean cultural policy, isolating single-site case studies is not the only analytical frame for exploring national cultural policies. Stepping back from the specificities of Psy and 'Gangnam Style', we can see a familiar process of (economic) instrumentalisation at work, as the state capitalises on its cultural industries. Looking beyond specificity and attempting to generalise and compare national cultural policies can therefore be seen as another key approach in policymaking and analysis.

VARIATIONS ON A THEME

In our discussion of typologies and models of national cultural policy earlier in this chapter, an issue we did not really pursue was the use of such classificatory systems for comparative analysis. Yet when we scan the literature we find numerous examples of comparison between nations, some of which draw explicitly on the typologies sketched earlier (e.g. Ulldemolins and Arostegui 2013). And this makes perfect sense: following the 'descriptive literature' of single-site case studies, an obvious next step is comparative work. Yet we also find plenty of cautionary tales and warnings about the folly or impossibility of comparative research. Dave O'Brien (2013: 37) justifies his exclusive focus on the UK by highlighting the 'difficulties of doing comparative policy work' (though he doesn't elaborate); serial typologist Kevin Mulcahy is equally blunt:

> It is as difficult as it is risky to offer even the most tentative general-izations about comparative public policymaking. Cultural policies are particularly enmeshed with national histories and political cultures.
>
> (Mulcahy 2000: 165)

And in a recent book review, Jeremy Ahearne (2013: 642) similarly alludes to 'the difficulties of cross-national comparison' before attempting to do this by reading *across* the various national case studies presented in the book he's reviewing (Poirrier 2011), concluding that they offer 'variants of a similar story'. Mulcahy concludes something similar, spotting three consistent trends even across the seemingly diverse national contexts he surveys: increasing decentralisation, increasing cultural particularism, increased market-isation. Such comparative reading is not only happening in cultural policy research; Andreas Wiesand (2002: 370) recounts increasing interest in comparison among policymakers, too, noting how, over the past 30–40 years, policymakers in Europe 'became increasingly curious about what their neighbours were up to and how they fared in comparison with them'. This little phrase is very telling: for policymakers, comparison means measuring 'success' – it is at least in part competitive. But it is also emulative: curiosity about one's neighbours, especially if they are faring better, can lead to copying. As discussed in Chapter 3, cultural policies are mobile, they are transferrable from one place to another – they tour. The global travels of creative industries discourse and policy has been perhaps the most discussed exemplar – if that is the right word, given that such discussions are often critical of the 'disembedded' transplant of such policy to very different national (and local) contexts (Cunningham 2009; Wang 2004).

Such travelling policy returns us to a question we hinted at earlier: are we to read national cultural policy as only, or mainly, concerned with the inner workings of the nation – is it 'internal' cultural policy (Ahearne 2009)? Or is there always an 'external' dimension – the use of national cultural policy on an international stage? In some cases, such as cultural diplomacy (see Chapter 6), cultural policy is explicitly externally directed. But we might argue that in the case of national cultural policy, the internal/external distinction can be hard to maintain, not least given the neighbourly comparison noted above. To return to creative industries policy for a moment: when the Labour government seized on ideas of 'Creative Britain' and 'Cool Britannia', who were they addressing? Were they telling British people how creative and cool they are, or telling the rest of the world? The answer can only be: *both*. National cultural policy can be internal and external, yet these two roles are often in tension (Minnaert 2014). As Wang (2004) puts it, it is always important to read national cultural policy *relationally* – an important shift in terminology. Relational analysis does not slide into easy comparison – or uneasy comparison for that matter – but instead considers both specificity and connection, and works across scales.

'BEYOND' THE NATION

Our tour of national cultural policy has to end by undermining the focus that has come before. For while, as Mark Schuster (2002: 181) writes, 'the national level ... is the most natural entry point for researchers and policy analysts moving into the field for the first time', the naturalness of the scale of the nation is increasingly being challenged, both in research and in policy-making. The primacy of the nation as the 'atom of analysis', as Monica Sassatelli (2002: 439) puts it, is being undermined from above and below as new units and targets of cultural policy come into focus. Here we need to attend to both subnational and supranational scales; for if, in countries like the USA, it is the former *'where the action is'* (Schuster 2002), then in other parts of the world, such as the nations of Europe, the latter is becoming a more significant operating scale for cultural policy and its analysis. Of course, these two forms of regional scale exist in relational interaction with the nation: questions of devolution or decentralisation only make sense in relation to the nation that is being devolved or decentralised, just as new supranational formations like the EU are still composed of nations – nations whose stance on Europeanisation (or other similar forms of supranational regional aggregation) exhibits sometimes extreme variance.

SUBNATIONAL CULTURAL POLICY

Chapter 4 deals with cultural policy at the urban scale; the jump from that to the national scale in this chapter leapfrogs over what can be very important policy formations at the subnational scale. In the USA, the relations between the national (federal) and subnational (state) scales bring this out very clearly.[2] Mark Schuster (2002) focusses in on US state-level cultural policy, arguing that in the US context (but, he suggests, relevant elsewhere, even beyond nations with federal structures), this is a neglected but vital scale for policy analysis. In a subsequent detailed study of one US state (Washington), Schuster and his team present a rich account of the 'ecology' of cultural policy at subnational (state) level (Schuster 2003). This study confirms that the subnational scale is indeed 'where the action is'. As Schuster (2003: 4) argues, 'direct support for the arts at state level is now – and has been for some time – a more important source of direct government aid to the arts than is direct support at the federal level'. Of course, despite Schuster's note about broader applicability, the USA is a distinctive case, with the balance between federal and state government articulated in a distinctive way. Yet he is right to urge us to shift our attention, not least because even national-level cultural policies are implemented on the ground at subnational, regional and local levels. Add to this the increasing tendency in many nations towards forms of devolution and decentralisation, and we can clearly see the subnational scale as a key player and a key unit of analysis. As Schuster puts it:

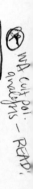

> The move towards delegation, devolution, and centralization in government policy making and implementation had made it more important to understand how policy actually plays out at the lower levels of government.
>
> (Schuster 2003: 5)

And such moves have often been acutely felt in cultural policy (Selwood 2010). Noboku Kawashima (1997: 341) has commented that 'decentralisation has assumed the status of a norm in cultural policy in many nations', and delineates three main forms of decentralising: cultural, fiscal and political. The former refers to the 'fair' or 'equal' distribution of culture to the population and so is concerned with questions of access and participation. Kawashima notes that a key mechanism is the spatial diffusion of cultural institutions or resources. Fiscal decentralisation refers to the spatial diffusion of money: the equalising of public expenditure (often to offset criticism of metropolitan bias) and the rebalancing of the national and subnational financial contribution to supporting culture. It may also refer to attempts to rebalance public subsidy for different cultural sectors. Lastly, political decentralisation concerns decision-making and implementation. This may mean devolution to non-government bodies or redistribution between national and subnational bodies – the arm's-length principle can be seen as a form of political decentralisation, as can the 'regionalisation' or 'localisation' of cultural policy (though this might be better thought of as deconcentration). Kawashima writes that decentralisation has become normative: in policy circles it is assumed to be 'a good thing' and a noble policy ambition. However, case studies of policy formations often reveal forms of *de facto* decentralisation, often as a result of the lack of national cultural policy – as discussed in the cases of Spain (Bonet and Negrier 2010) and Italy (Montalto 2010), for example. In the latter case, a recent attempted reversal of decentralisation, in the form of a national policy initiative aimed at young artists, is argued to have misfired because it is at odds with the *de facto* devolution that had previously shaped Italy's cultural landscape.

In the case of the UK, the balance of national, regional and local scales in terms of cultural policy has seen a number of shifts over time. Sara Selwood (2010: 1) comments that 'the UK has witnessed simultaneously the decline of regionalism and the rise of devolved governments that are experimenting with cultural policy as one of their first exercises in independence from London'. Commenting on the decline in regionalism in the arts, Clive Gray (2000) describes a political struggle between the 'centre' and the regions, laying out the history of the regional scale in UK arts policy, from the formation of the regional arts associations in the 1950s – and their ambivalent relationship to the central Arts Council of Great Britain – to their replacement with ten regional arts boards in 1990, which were more closely articulated to ACGB, a move seen by Gray as evidence of greater centralisation (though the 1980s had seen repeated criticism of the neglect of the regions by ACGB). By the early 1990s, ACGB had undergone devolution to its English, Welsh, Northern Irish and Scottish constituencies, while the DNH was established as the UK's first 'cultural ministry' in 1992, morphing into the DCMS in 1997. In 2002, the RABs were reabsorbed back into ACE and converted into nine regional offices which were coterminous with the regional development agencies (RDAs), which were themselves established in 1998. Post-1997, the Labour government pursued various forms of regional agenda, including in 2004 the establishment of regional cultural consortiums (RCCs) which also mapped onto the RDAs and the 'new' geography of the English regions (Lutz 2006; Ravenscroft 2005). In 2008 it was announced that the RCCs would be closed down, with national arts bodies and RDAs overseeing culture in the regions from now on. The RDAs were abolished in 2012. Meanwhile, ACE reorganised its regional presence and today has five area councils, covering London, the North, the Midlands, the South West and the South East.

Stepping back from the detail of this story, we can see the regions coming in and out of focus, rising and falling in prominence. Geographers have long considered regions to be constructed spaces that exist relationally – in relation to other regions, but also to other scales (e.g. Gilbert 1988). The same can be said of nations, of course – and in some cases already discussed, such as those of Spain and Italy, the regional scale has a longer history and deeper meaning (in terms of people's identities) than the nation. Both nation and region are 'fictions', so making regions matter in policy terms can be seen as a discursive strategy 'to make stable the inherently unstable meanings of regions' (Ravenscroft 2005: 164). Bodies like RCCs and RDAs 'perform' the region, helping to make it 'real'. While the UK context is somewhat different from the USA – the English regions are certainly 'fuzzier' than the US states – both cases tell us a relational story: the subnational scale only makes sense when read in relation to the national (and the local). The same must be said for scales 'above' the nation, of course.

"subvationalism"

SUPRANATIONAL CULTURAL POLICY *"supranational"*

Chapter 6 focusses on the interplay between cultural policy and globalisation, so our discussion here will be brief, and will try not to stray too far into global territory. Nevertheless, alongside processes of subnationalisation we can identify significant processes of supranationalisation – the bringing together of nations into agglomerations, an obvious example being the European Union. As Monica Sassatelli (2002) writes, the forging of European identity in the EU has been a major cultural policy target, given the primacy of culture in questions of identity. Formalised in the Treaty of Maastricht (and later amended), the 'cultural' role of the EU is to 'contribute to the flowering of the cultures of member states, while respecting their national and regional diversity and at the same time bringing the common cultural heritage to the fore' (quoted in Sassatelli 2002: 440). There are a number of tensions in this statement; for our discussion here, the one to think about is the scalar tension between national and 'common' (i.e. European) culture: EU cultural policy as expressed here foregrounds the national – encouraging it to flower and respecting its diversity – while at the same time a common culture (or, more accurately, a common *cultural heritage*) is to be highlighted. The notion of a common European heritage provides a historical glue to bind contemporary Europe together without forcing cultural homogeneity. But what is the common cultural heritage of Europe?

Sassatelli interrogates arguably the most prominent EU intervention in the area of culture, the European Capital of Culture (ECoC) programme (see also Chapter 4). Focussing on the 2000 programme, she shows the repeated articulation of the Europeanness of ECoC among the official ECoC documents. The 2000 programme is significant in that nine cities were chosen as co-hosts in a millennial special: Brussels, Krakow and Prague from 'Central' Europe, Bergen, Reykjavik and Helsinki from the 'North', and Avignon, Bologna and Santiago de Compostela from the 'South' (note the regional naming avoids the more contentious labels of 'Western' and 'Eastern' Europe). This nine-city programme represents the intention (and the difficulties) of the Maastricht statement; indeed, the extent to which the ECoC programme is

Is culture relational?

able to promote flowering, diversity and common heritage is an on-going question.

Thomas Perrin (2010) considers a different aspect of EU cultural policy – the formation of cross-border 'Euroregions' that transcend national boundaries and bridge national divides. Looking in particular at the Pyrénées-Méditerranée and Grande-Région, he explores inter-territorial cultural policy activity, sensing a new regional agenda (though he also finds on-the-ground impediments such as transport linkages and national differences in cultural workers' rights). So here we have inter-territorial regions nested within the supranational EU region: it might be tempting to claim these inter-territorial regions as somehow more 'natural', but to do so would be to lapse into a dangerous cultural essentialism. As with other cross-border initiatives in the EU, such as those around health care,[3] what's interesting here is the interplay between different forms of region and the nation. Clearly, a series of relational, intersecting scales or geographies which both connect to and transcend the scale of the nation and the geography of its borders can be observed, posing opportunities and also challenges for cultural policymaking and analysis.

CONCLUSIONS

At the time of writing, the French government had announced delaying its proposed new smartphone tax until 2015; Maria Miller, meanwhile, is mired in the issue of press regulation in the wake of the Leveson Inquiry into phone hacking by newspaper reporters. The terrain of national cultural policy is ever-shifting, therefore: and while our closing focus on subnational and supra-national scales might have suggested the disappearance of the nation – a common discourse in the context of globalisation, as we shall see – we do not want to suggest that the nation is disappearing in terms of cultural policy, or at least disappearing from cultural policy studies (Turner 2014). National governments remain key players in cultural policy, and cultural policy retains its role in shaping the nation. Our analysis in this chapter aims, rather, to point up the relational dimension of cultural policy – policy which remains territorially defined, though our understanding of territory and territoriality has also shifted, become relational. As with the ongoing national conversation about the role and value of the BBC, or the DCMS for that matter, national cultural policy is a form of banal nationalism: it defines and expresses national character, it speaks internally and externally, to the nation and to the world. Even today it represents the autobiography of the nation.

NOTES

1 The arm's length of the UGC was itself shortened into non-existence under the Thatcher government; see Warnock 2000.
2 In his discussion of US subnational policy, Schuster (2002) notes potential confusion over the use of the term 'state', which in the US context means one of the 50 states that federate to make up the US, whereas in other contexts the term 'state' is a synonym for national government or for the nation. We reproduce this confusion in this chapter!
3 See http://ec.europa.eu/health/cross_border_care/policy/index_en.htm.

REFERENCES AND FURTHER READING

Ahearne, J. (2009) 'Cultural policy explicit and implicit: a distinction and some uses', International Journal of Cultural Policy, 15(2): 141–53.
——(2013) Review of Pour une histoire des politiques culturelles dans le monde, 1945–2011, edited by Philippe Poirrier, International Journal of Cultural Policy, 19(5): 641–5.
Alasuutari, P. (2001) 'Arts, entertainment, culture, and nation', Cultural Studies <=> Critical Methodologies, 1(2): 157–84.
Alexander, V. (2008) 'Cultural organizations and the state: art and state support in contemporary Britain', Sociology Compass, 2(5): 1416–30.
Anderson, B. (1991) Imagined Communities: Reflections on the Origin and Spread of Nationalism, London: Verso.
Auerbach, J. (1999) The Great Exhibition of 1851: a Nation on Display, New Haven CT: Yale University Press.
Billig, M. (1995) Banal Nationalism, London: Sage.
Bonet, L. and Negrier, E. (2010) 'Cultural Policy in Spain: processes and dialectics', Cultural Trends, 19(1/2): 41–52.
Bordat, E. (2013) 'Institutionalization and change in cultural policy: CONACULTA and cultural policy in Mexico (1988–2006)', International Journal of Cultural Policy, 19(2): 222–48.
Chartrand, H. and McCaughey, C. (1989) 'The arm's length principle and the arts: an international perspective – past, present, and future', in M. Cummings and M. Schuster (eds), Who's to Pay for the Arts? The International Search for Models of Support, New York: ACA Books.

Conekin, B. (2003) 'The Autobiography of a Nation': the 1951 Festival of Britain, Manchester: Manchester University Press.

Craik, J., McAllister, L. and Davis, G. (2003) 'Paradoxes and contradictions in government approaches to contemporary cultural policy: an Australian perspective', International Journal of Cultural Policy, 9(1): 17–33.

Cummings, M. and Schuster, M. (eds) (1989), Who's to Pay for the Arts? The International Search for Models of Support, New York: ACA Books.

Cunningham, S. (2009) 'Trojan Horse or Rorschach Blot? Creative industries discourse around the world', International Journal of Cultural Policy, 15(4): 375–86.

DeVereaux, C. and Griffin, M. (2013) Narrative, Identity, and the Map of Cultural Policy: Once upon a Time in a Globalized World, Farnham: Ashgate.

Dickinson, M. and Harvey, S. (2005) 'Film policy in the United Kingdom: New Labour at the movies', The Political Quarterly, 76(3): 420–9.

Dueland, P. (2008) 'Nordic cultural policies: a critical review', International Journal of Cultural Policy, 14(1): 7–24.

Gilbert, A. (1988) 'The new regional geography in English and French-speaking countries', Progress in Human Geography, 12(2): 208–28.

Gray, C. (2000) The Politics of the Arts in Britain, Basingstoke: Macmillan.

——(2008) 'Arts Council England and public value: a critical review', International Journal of Cultural Policy, 14(2): 209–14.

Gray, C. and Wingfield, M. (2011) 'Are governmental culture departments important? An empirical investigation', International Journal of Cultural Policy, 17(5): 590–604.

Häyrynen, S. (2013) 'A centralised market orientation: the implicit determinants of Finnish cultural policy in 1990–2010', International Journal of Cultural Policy, 19(5): 623–40.

Hewison, R. (1995) Culture and Consensus: England, Art and Politics since 1945, London: Methuen.

Higgins, C. (2013) 'Maria Miller's last-chance saloon', The Guardian culture blog. Available at www.guardian.co.uk/culture/charlottehigginsblog (accessed 12/04/14).

Hobsbawn, E. and Ranger, T. (eds) (1983) The Invention of Tradition, Cambridge: Cambridge University Press.

Kawashima, N. (1997) 'Theorising decentralisation in cultural policy: concepts, values and strategies', Cultural Policy, 3(2): 341–59.

——(2012) 'Corporate support for the arts in Japan: beyond emulation of the Western models', International Journal of Cultural Policy, 18(3): 295–307.

Kong, L. (2000) 'Cultural policy in Singapore: negotiating economic and socio-cultural agendas', Geoforum, 31(3): 409–24.

Kwon, S.-H. and Kim, J. (2013) 'The cultural industry policies of the Korean government and the Korean Wave', International Journal of Cultural Policy, online first.

Looseley, D. (1995) The Politics of Fun: Cultural Policy and Debate in Contemporary France, Oxford: Berg.

——(2011) 'Notions of popular culture in cultural policy: a comparative history of France and Britain', *International Journal of Cultural Policy*, 17(4), 365–79.

Lutz, J. (2006) 'Extending the cultural research infrastructure: the rise of the Regional Cultural Consortiums in England', *Cultural Trends*, 15(1): 19–44.

MacNeill, K., Lye, J. and Caulfield, P. (2013) 'Politics, reviews and support for the arts: an analysis of government expenditures on the arts in Australia from 1967 to 2009', *Australian Review of Public Affairs*, 12(1): 1–19.

Madden, C. (2009) *The Independence of Government Arts Funding: a Review*, Sydney: IFACCA.

Magor, M. and Schlesinger, P. (2009) '"For this relief, much thanks": taxation, film policy and the UK government', *Screen*, 50(3): 299–317.

Mangset, P., Kangas, A., Skot-Hansen, D. and Vestheim, G. (2008) 'Editors' introduction: Nordic cultural policy', *International Journal of Cultural Policy*, 14(1): 1–5.

Matarasso, F. and Landry, C. (1999) *Balancing Act: Twenty-one Strategic Dilemmas in Cultural Policy*, Strasbourg: Council of Europe.

McGuigan, J. (2004) *Rethinking Cultural Policy*, Maidenhead: Open University Press.

McNeill, D. and Tewdwr-Jones, M. (2003) 'Architecture, banal nationalism and re-territorialization', *International Journal of Urban and Regional Research*, 27(3): 738–43.

Miller, T. and Yudice, G. (2002) *Cultural Policy*, London: Sage.

Minnaert, T. (2014) 'Footprint or fingerprint: international cultural policy as identity policy', *International Journal of Cultural Policy*, online first.

Montalto, V. (2010) 'Decentralization and devolution in Italian cultural policies: how micro-practices should inspire macro-policies', *Cultural Trends*, 19(1/2): 15–25.

Mulcahy, K. (1987) 'Government and the arts in the United States', in M. Cummings and R. Katz (eds), *The Patron State: Government and the Arts in Europe, North America, and Japan*, New York: Oxford University Press.

——(2000) 'The government and cultural patronage: a comparative analysis of cultural patronage in the United States, France, Norway, and Canada', in J. Cherbo and M. Wyszomirski (eds), *The Public Life of the Arts in America*, New Brunswick NJ: Rutgers University Press.

——(2006) 'Cultural policy', in B. G. Peters and J. Pierre (eds), *Handbook of Public Policy*, London: Sage.

Netzer, D. (1978) *The Subsidized Muse: Public Support for the Arts in the United States*, Cambridge: Cambridge University Press.

Newsinger, J. (2012) 'British film policy in an age of austerity', *Journal of British Cinema and Television*, 9(1): 133–44.

O'Brien, D. (2012) 'Drowning the deadweight in the rhetoric of economism: what sport policy, free swimming, and the EMA tell us about public services after the crash', *Public Administration*, 81(1): 69–82.

——(2013) *Cultural Policy: Management, Value and Modernity in the Creative Industries*, London: Routledge.

Perrin, T. (2010) 'Inter-territoriality as a new trend in cultural policy? The case of Euroregions', *Cultural Trends*, 19(1/2): 125–39.

Poirrier, P. (ed.) (2011) *Pour une Histoire des Politiques Culturelles dans le Monde, 1945–2011*, Paris: La Documentation Francaise.

Quinn, R. (1997) 'Distance or intimacy? The arm's length principle, the British government and the Arts Council of Great Britain', *International Journal of Cultural Policy*, 4(1): 127–60.

Ravenscroft, N. (2005) 'Developing the cultural agenda: the socio-spatial dimensions of the Regional Cultural Strategies in England', *Space and Polity*, 9(2): 149–66.

Ridley, F. (1987) 'Tradition, change, and crisis in Great Britain', in M. Cummings and R. Katz (eds), *The Patron State: Government and the Arts in Europe, North America, and Japan*, New York: Oxford University Press.

Robins, K. (2007) 'Transnational cultural policy and European cosmopolitanism', *Cultural Politics*, 3(2): 147–74.

Roche, M. (2000) *Mega-events and Modernity: Olympics and Expos in the Growth of Global Culture*, London: Routledge.

Sassatelli, M. (2002) 'Imagined Europe: the shaping of a European cultural identity through EU cultural policy', *European Journal of Social Theory*, 5(4): 435–51.

Schuster, J. M. (1985) *Supporting the Arts: an International Comparative Study*, Cambridge MA: MIT Press.

——(2002) 'Sub-national Cultural Policy – where the action is: mapping state cultural policy in the United States', *International Journal of Cultural Policy*, 8(2): 181–96.

Schuster, J. M. (ed.) (2003) *Mapping State Cultural Policy: the State of Washington*, Chicago IL: University of Chicago Cultural Policy Center.

Selwood, S. (2010) 'Centre/periphery: devolution/federalism: new trends in cultural policy', *Cultural Trends*, 19(1/2): 1–2.

Turner, G. (2014) 'Culture, politics and the cultural industries: reviving a critical agenda', in K. Oakley and J. O'Connor (eds) *The Routledge Companion to the Cultural Industries*, London: Routledge.

Ulldemolins, J. and Arostegui, A. (2013) 'The governance of national cultural organisations: comparative study of performance contracts with the main cultural organisations in Enlgand, France and Catalonia (Spain)', *International Journal of Cultural Policy*, 19(2): 249–69.

Wang, J. (2004) 'The global reach of a new discourse: how far can "creative industries" travel?' *International Journal of Cultural Studies*, 7(1): 9–19.

Warnock, M. (2000) 'Introduction', in M. Wallinger and M. Warnock (eds) *Art for All? Their Policies and Our Culture*, London: PEER.

Wiesand, A. (2002) 'Comparative cultural policy research in Europe: a change of paradigm', *Canadian Journal of Communication*, 27(3): 369–78.

Williams, R. (1979) 'The Arts Council', *The Political Quarterly*, 50(2): 157–71.

——(1984) 'State, culture and beyond', in L. Apignanesi (ed.), *Culture and the State*, London: ICA.

Willsher, K. (2013) 'Francois Hollande considers tax on smartphones and laptops', *The Guardian*, 13 May. Available at www.theguardian.com/world/2013/may/13/francois-hollande-tax-iphones-laptops (accessed 14/04/14).

Worpole, K. (2001) 'Cartels and lotteries: heritage and cultural policy in Britain', in D. Morely and K. Robins (eds) *British Cultural Studies: Geography, Nationality and Identity*, Oxford: Oxford University Press.

Zorba, M. (2009) 'Conceptualizing Greek cultural policy: the non-democratization of public culture', *International Journal of Cultural Policy*, 15(3): 245–59.

6

INTERNATIONAL CULTURAL POLICY

The internationalisation of the world economy provides a fundamental context for the production, consumption and distribution of
cultural products and, thanks to the growth of digital technology,
more and more of them find audiences far from home. World
trade in cultural goods and services more than doubled between
2002 and 2011, reaching US$ 624bn in 2011 (UNESCO 2013).
Yet policy to some degree lags behind this development. As we
have discussed in previous chapters, despite its alleged decline in
importance, the nation-state remains the prime mover in cultural
regulation and indeed support, while the city is increasingly the
site of policy innovation. Global trade is often where the tension
between economics and culture becomes most apparent, yet disputes
at this level are still primarily between nation-states. These include
questions such as what, if anything, is to be done about the US
dominance of international cultural trade? How to preserve the
French language or the Korean film industry?

Nonetheless, the twentieth century has seen the rise of both
regional policy institutions with a cultural remit, such as

MERCOSUR[1] or the European Union, and global ones, such as the United Nations (UN) and its agencies, for example the UN Educational, Scientific and Cultural Organisation (UNESCO) and the UN Conference on Trade and Development (UNCTAD). These organisations have shaped cultural policy and may do even more in future, though the development of effective international policy organisations is uneven, as it is in many other policy spheres. Yet despite the number of media and communications scholars who have written on aspects of globalisation and on topics such as trade wars and cultural imperialism (Herman and McChesney 1997; Miller *et al.* 2004; Tunstall 1994), as Paschalidis (2009) has argued, cultural policy research has tended to avoid the topic of international cultural policy (ICP), preferring to leave it to scholars of diplomacy or foreign relations.

David Throsby has usefully summarised areas where culture engages with the economy internationally:

- international trade in tangible cultural products such as artworks, books, CDs, etc.;
- international trade in intellectual property rights relating to intangible cultural commodities such as television programmes, movies, digitised music, etc.;
- international labour movements affecting the cultural industries such as the mobility of artists;
- international cultural exchanges such as touring by performing companies, the circulation of artworks and artefacts on loan between museums and galleries, etc.;
- international cultural diplomacy and the exercise of 'soft power';
- international cultural tourism.

(Throsby 2010: 157)

To this we can add policy transfer and the travels of policy discourse such as that of the 'creative economy', which increasingly structures policy approaches across a range of contexts (see Chapter 3). Here we consider most of the issues mentioned above, though we focus on those where the primary question is a *policy* question, such as trade or diplomacy, rather than, say, cultural tourism (a fascinating area where many of us encounter the culture of other nations for the first time, but not one where cultural policy plays a particularly important role).

The discussion of global cultural policy is just one part of the complex relationship between culture and globalisation. On the one hand, culture (and cultural policy) can be seen to be facilitating forms of globalisation, particularly as digital networks allow the rapid exchange of new cultural products or expressions. But cultural policy can also be seen in reaction to globalisation, such as in forms of economic protectionism; while localised cultural scenes continue to thrive, often in response to the perceived blandness of 'globalised' cultural production.

The idea of globalisation is a highly contested one, not only in its effects but also the degree to which it is an accurate depiction of the current world economy. This chapter will not discuss in any detail the contending positions over the degree to which the world economy is globalised; they have been well-summarised by Held and his colleagues (Held 2005; Held and McGrew 2000). While we seek to avoid some of the more excessive claims about globalisation, particularly the degree to which it represents a novel phenomenon, we do accept that there is increasing integration of the world economy, driven by deregulatory policy regimes, the emergence of global consumer markets and the growth of digital communications, among other factors. This is not a one-way process of 'Westernisation', and there is no inevitability about its continuation. Instead what we are witnessing is the development of a multi-polar world in which culture plays an increasingly important role, economically and socially, and where policy regimes are often struggling to adapt, but one which also remains a battleground for competing ideas and visions of the role and importance of culture.

CULTURAL TRADE

Cultural goods are perhaps amongst the earliest forms of trade, and the geographic patterns that cultural trade follow tell us much about world history. In her account of treaties and the international art market, Braman (2008) notes that in terms of the global market for fine art, a distinction is made between three types of state: source countries, buyer counties and *entrepôt* countries. While 'source' countries vary – from the French and Italian homes of European 'Old Masters' to ancient art from Egypt or Ethiopia and contemporary art from anywhere – buyers are concentrated in far fewer places. The buyer market is dominated by the UK and the USA (home of international art auctioneers such as Sotheby's and Christies) and by newly wealthy economies such as China. *Entrepôt* countries are those which make it possible to transfer art from producers to buyers – sometimes dubiously, as when art treasures have been stolen from collections or otherwise obtained illegally.

Braman describes how international treaties increasingly govern this global market as nation-states have struggled to keep up with developments, particularly where power relations between states are highly unequal. She gives the example of Cambodia, which, following the 1996 peace treaty between the Khmer Rouge and the Cambodian government, began the slow task of clearing the 4–5 million landmines from its territory. As it did so, residents began to unearth cultural artefacts, some of which have value in the global art market, and in some cases sought to export them. As she describes, in a state already over-burdened by the need to clear landmines and undertake basic development, there was little hope of having the resources to protect its own heritage.

As this suggests, cultural goods are often among the more problematic aspects of international trade negotiations, 'providing a paradigm case of the conflict between economic values and cultural values', as Throsby (2010: 158) puts it. As cultural goods, both tangible and intangible, are frequently entangled with and expressive of localised identities, beliefs and sense of place, this is hardly surprising. The rhetoric of 'free trade' often sits uneasily with talk of cultural goods and services, even for those who are not opposed to it for other classes of goods. In some cases, this concern is about the commodification of previously uncommodified goods and the threat that this might pose. Cultural tourism offers many examples of this, such as when sacred sites like Uluru in central Australia become the venue for adventure tourists. In this case, the cultural and spiritual value of the site for one group of people is threatened by the fact that another group of people simply regard it as a large rock that might be fun to climb.

Other examples concern crowding out – the threat to minority languages from dominant national or international languages, for example, which often warrants explicit state intervention in minority language such as Welsh or Catalan. In other cases the issue is one of voice and identity: given that we learn so much about the world through our consumption of cultural goods, why is those outside the origin countries rarely see Iranian television, Argentinean films or translated Dutch novels? The success of Scandinavian crime fiction, both on TV and in novel form in the UK and other countries in recent years suggests that there often is a market for cultural products in translation, despite conventional wisdom that, for instance, TV viewers would not read subtitles.

This issue is often referred to by the shorthand of the 'cultural exception', which refers to attempts to treat cultural goods differently within international trade treaties as a way of recognising they have more than economic importance (see Chapter 5). Throsby (2010) makes the important point that such arguments, though often couched in economic language, in fact mix cultural, ideological and ethical arguments alongside those of trade. He summarises these arguments thus:

- cultural products are vehicles for symbolic messages that transcend products' purely commercial value, such that normal market processes will not be capable of fully capturing their value to society;
- cultural products are essential to the expression of national identity and hence their protection is warranted in the public interest;
- a wide range of domestically produced cultural products is important for cultural diversity;
- cultural products may be subject to unfair competition from the dumping of cheap imports and are therefore worthy of protection under competition law;
- industries producing cultural products may be eligible for infant industry protection if their growth prospects indicate eventual self-sufficiency.

(Thorsby 2010: 160)

A glance at this list gives us a deep sense of how culture is 'different', or maybe regarded differently, from other sorts of goods. After all, the 'dumping' of imports[2] may occur in other parts of the market, or infant industries in agriculture or electronics may also be threatened by imports. WTO rules can be invoked here as well, but in these cases the arguments are largely economic – for example, developing an electronics industry can provide jobs and economic growth. But questions of identity, self-recognition or national cohesion are rarely invoked in the cases of other sorts of goods, while in the case of culture, despite the best efforts of some economists, they are routinely seen as important.

For the most part, global cultural trade has been dominated by the USA, particularly in popular culture, film, TV and music (Shuker 2003), and resistance to this has often defined itself as resistance to 'cultural imperialism' (Hesmondhalgh 2013; Lewis and Miller 2003; Tunstall 1994). This particular term has somewhat fallen out of favour in recent years. It was criticised for accepting the idea of 'national' cultures as a given, rather than recognising the variety of cultures within the nation, and for the rather dubious elision of the idea of 'local' with 'authentic' and 'imported' with commercial or inauthentic. In addition, as Hesmondhalgh (2013) argues, a focus on US domination neglects some regional forms of domination: the prominence of Egyptian TV in the Arabic-speaking world, for example, or of Mexican and Brazilian TV in Latin America.

In what he prefers to call 'internationalisation' rather than 'globalisation', Hesmondhalgh (2013) provides a useful analysis of arguments about cultural imperialism in three cultural industries: television, film and popular music. His argument is that while a simplistic account of cultural imperialism, particularly if read purely as US cultural imperialism, cannot capture the full reality of cultural production and trade, we should not rush to assume that the rise in popularity of Korean pop music or Arabic news journalism means that all concerns about power and dominance in cultural trade are at an end. The USA remains the world's dominant cultural producer: of the 31 largest cinema-going territories in the world, US films accounted for more than 50 per cent of admissions in 24 of them. And while popular music with its lower production costs has many more significant centres of production than the film industry, and indeed is often associated with particular urban scenes, US and UK acts continue to dominate global sales to an extraordinary extent.

Opposition to the dominance of imported popular culture is easily mocked as elitist, but as Throsby (2010: 162) notes, in a world of highly unequal economic power, 'it was market dominance by the transglobal corporate giants in the audio-visual media industries that was seen as the main cause for concern', not necessarily Americanisation or loss of 'authenticity'. This dominance is rarely absolute – demand for locally relevant content in national languages invariably survives, with most consumers having access to a mix of imported and local content and to hybrids of both – but while the idea of cultural imperialism has become less fashionable, the dominance of global media production has not become of any less concern.

The post-Second World War years saw the development of a variety of global bodies such as the United Nations, as well as the development of an integrated global trading system. Central to this was the General Agreement on Tariffs and Trade (GATT), the aims of which were to reduce import tariffs, increase world trade, and thus speed up the process of global capitalist development. Though the principle behind the GATT was supposed to be equal treatment for each nation, the inequality in development terms at the time the treaty was signed ensured that it would effectively favour more developed nations. The provisions of the GATT were challenged by developing countries for a variety of reasons from the start (Braman 2008), but it was developed countries, notably France and Canada, that are generally associated with arguing for the cultural exception (see Chapter 5 for the contemporary story of this phenomenon). Although France was a signatory to many of these agreements, it consistently sought an exception for cultural goods – particularly in the audio-visual sphere, where Hollywood was so dominant. Article IV of the GATT allowed countries to impose screen quotas at the cinema in order to protect domestic film industries, the majority of which to this day would not survive without public support of some sort (Feigenbaum 2010).

The successor body to the GATT is the World Trade Organisation (WTO), in which similar debates have continued and intensified. In the period leading up to its formation in 1993, France and

Canada argued for a continued cultural exception that would exempt audio-visual goods from WTO processes. When the USA forced trade in services as well as goods onto the agenda of the GATT, in the early 1980s, alarm bells began ringing. In a now-famous speech to a UNESCO conference in Mexico in 1982, the then-French cultural minister Jack Lang warned of the dangers of American cultural imperialism and the erosion of autonomy and loss of identity, suffered not only by developing countries but also by developed nations such as France. The French response was to double cultural spending, to try and boost local production and also to fight against 'free trade' in culture; in a sense enacting its own form of cultural exception. As McGuigan (2004) comments, France was generally keen to go along with the flow of neoliberalism in trade talks when it concerned pharmaceuticals or aerospace engineering, but not when it came to culture.

While a *general* cultural exception was not accepted by the WTO, the resulting treaty, the General Agreement on Trade in Services (GATS), did allow for some flexibility in cultural trade, and signatories could decide whether to apply exceptions to audio-visual goods (though few chose to do so). These arrangements were intended to be temporary; further liberalisation of world trade, including trade in cultural goods, was envisaged, but the current round of world trade talks, the so-called Doha Round (launched in 2001 in Doha, Qatar) is still to be completed more than a decade later, so no further progress has been made in addressing this issue at WTO level.

CULTURAL DIVERSITY

While arguments about cultural trade and cultural exemptions continue to rage, both sides frequently evoke the notion of increasing cultural diversity as support for their version of the debate. For free marketeers like Tyler Cowen (1998) the market is the best guarantor of a diverse range of cultural production; opponents argue that it simply results in market domination by a small number of large producers. This confirms at least that cultural diversity is an important notion and one that we see held up as a goal at a variety of spatial and policy levels.

But why is it so? Throsby (2010) outlines some of the reasons for valuing cultural diversity, often in a direct parallel with notions of biodiversity. Diversity, he argues, is valued for its own sake, much as the diversity of species is – the ability to see it from many different viewpoints simply makes the world more interesting. Second, greater diversity breeds greater diversity – if cultures exist in isolation they are more likely to stagnate, and having a greater variety of resources to draw on in the first place can lead to greater innovation. We know that cultural production can appear, in strictly economic terms, as a wasteful enterprise, as many films, books, songs and videogames are required to generate a few 'hits', but it is the very abundance of cultural life than helps drive it. Finally he argues that cultural diversity is valuable 'because it keeps options open for the future' (Throsby 2010: 173); the extinction of cultural practices robs not just us in the present of the enjoyment of diverse cultural products, but future generations.

Since its inauguration, UNESCO has provided a focus for the discussion of cultural diversity, which it tends to represent both in anthropological and in symbolic cultural terms (see Chapter 1 for a discussion of this distinction), with different understandings of culture dominating at different periods. In its early years, in the 1950s and 1960s, UNESCO was concerned primarily with culture as arts policy, still the case in many countries (see Chapter 2), and only from the 1970s onwards, as culture became linked to a notion of 'development', did a more anthropological notion of culture come to the fore. Pyykkönen (2012) points out that this notion of diversity derives from earlier United Nations and UNESCO texts, in particular the Universal Declaration of Human Rights (United Nations, 1948) and the Universal Declaration on Cultural Diversity (UNESCO, 2001), which represent cultural diversity as fundamental for humankind, linking it to ideas of democracy and human rights, in a way that took its remit far beyond 'arts' policy.

In so doing, UNESCO helped question the hierarchical opposition of 'traditional' and 'modern' societies, often mapped onto a crude 'developing' and 'developed' country model that seems to suggest modernity is a one-way flow, from the Global North to the Global South, and furthermore (and erroneously) that developed, modern societies have no traditions. UNESCO's more fluid stance allows countries, particularly those emerging from colonialism, to reject a single path to 'modernity', one based on consumption of a 'global' culture, which often seemed to relegate them to a position purely as providers of traditional or folkloric culture.

The advantage of such a broad approach is that UNESCO can sometimes make arguments that other cultural policymakers have failed to pursue. In particular, the UNESCO report of the World Commission on Culture and Development, *Our Creative Diversity* (WCCD 1995), argued that an exclusive focus on economic development had led to a range of social, cultural and economic problems around the world as a result of the dominance of multinational cultural providers. To address this the Commission argued that 'there was a need to transcend economics, without abandoning it' (quoted in McGuigan 2004: 100).

While WTO talks seemed to be continuing in a broadly 'pro-market' direction, persistent concerns in a number of countries, in particular disagreements between the European Union and the WTO on broadcasting, as well as between Canada and the USA on tariffs on imported magazines, led to the formation of UNESCO's Convention on the Protection and Promotion of the Diversity of Cultural Expressions (generally referred to as the Cultural Diversity Convention), adopted in 2005. The aim of the Convention is to protect cultural expressions deemed 'at the risk of extinction, under serious threat, or others in need of urgent safeguarding' (quoted in Throsby 2010: 170).

The echo of language associated with the biological sphere is not coincidental; the argument is that a cultural form, once lost, may be impossible to recover and that this represents a profound, human loss – an 'extinction'. In stressing the importance of 'diversity' for maintaining a healthy cultural ecosystem, UNESCO was in a sense agreeing to defend the right of states to 'protect' their culture, even at a time when protectionism of any sort in economic terms was officially viewed as an avoidable evil. The only countries to vote against the Convention were the USA and Israel, so although France and Canada may have led the lobbying, the Cultural Diversity Convention clearly struck a chord even with those countries generally keen to promote free trade or maintain good relations with the USA.

UNESCO is always keen to stress that the Convention is about protecting diversity *of cultural expression*, not just culture – that it should be seen as not just about heritage protection but as something that has resonance in the contemporary world of cultural production. There is debate about how effective it is in this latter respect, as we shall see. As Throsby (2010) comments, protection in the case of the Convention includes safeguarding *vulnerable* cultural expressions. This can either refer directly to cultural artefacts, art works, and heritage sites (a classic understanding of 'protection', perhaps) or to the capacity to *produce* contemporary cultural goods, such as the right to protect domestic broadcasting, film production and publishing. However, the former interpretation is likely to be the easier one for nations to follow. While preserving heritage sites from water damage or attack by particular groups opposed to their content (as in the case of the recent attacks on the Sidi Yahya Mosque in Timbuktu, for example) might be difficult or even dangerous, it is likely to evoke relatively widespread political support.

Even outside of the Convention, public support can often be mobilised to stop the export of particular items of cultural heritage, despite the fact that they are not strictly speaking 'at risk' (at least not of ceasing to exist). In the case of the UK, for example, a set of conditions know as the Waverley Criteria is applied in cases where particular art work (paintings or sculptures – they are usually moveable art works for obvious reasons) can be exported. In this case the secretary of state for culture might be asked to consider:

- whether the item is connected to the history of national life of the country;
- if it is of outstanding aesthetic importance in general or for specific branches of learning, i.e. significant in the development of a particular arts form or industrial process.

In these cases the determination is made by an independent expert committee (an example of the 'arm's-length principle' at work, see Chapter 5), which may have to balance the rights of owners (who may want to sell artworks to the highest global bidder) over the need to protect the nation's heritage. This is a clear example of where what would otherwise be seen as uncontroversial in a capitalist society – the right of an owner to sell something they legally own – becomes constrained by the right of a community, in this case the nation, to retain something. Protecting diversity of contemporary cultural expression, however, may prove far more politically difficult, not only because contemporary cultural products have not yet had the time to develop the sense of connection to a way of life that historical products have; but more pertinently it may involve taking on large media or software corporations whose current activities could be seen to be reducing the potential for diverse cultural expression.

Despite its wide-ranging provisions, the Convention does not impose enforceable obligations on its signatories and the degree to which it can really protect democratic or localised cultural expression remains unclear. In addition, critics of the Convention (e.g. Pyykkönen 2012) argue that behind its rhetoric of protection, its overwhelming tendency is towards the commodification of culture and hence the development of a market for culture. A further complication is that most signatories are also members of the WTO, which remains a proponent of free trade, and the degree to which these two approaches can be reconciled is far from clear. However, in stressing the importance of cultural diversity and at least opening the door to a notion of values not just beyond economic growth but sometimes in conflict with it, UNESCO was offering a space for a new discourse of cultural development, just at a time when the 'creative economy' discourse was concentrating still further on culture's role in economic growth (see next section for further discussion of this issue).

The 2005 Cultural Diversity Convention explicitly recognises the distinction between economic and cultural values, asserts that both are important, and sets out a series of measures which can be developed at national or international level. These include measures on media diversity, the promotion of cultural exchange and partnerships, and the establishment of an International Fund for Cultural Diversity, which seeks to strengthen both the institutional infrastructure and the cultural industries of developing countries.

The reference to cultural industries above reminds us that the discourse of the 'creative economy' has been as influential at the level of international policymaking organisation as it has at national and urban level (Turner 2014). From the later 1990s the 'creative industries' idea began to achieve international traction (Cunningham 2009), including in the Global South, which might be assumed to have been hostile not only to the elision of culture and economics but also to a discourse so clearly fashioned in the Global North. But many countries – from Brazil to Senegal – have seen cultural industry-led development as holding out a great deal of promise, a chance for localised cultural expression to reach international audiences and, with the new digital technologies of satellite and the Internet, to develop media industries less dominated by the multinationals. In this sense, the argument was not dissimilar to that promoted by advocates in the Global North: that of 'creativity' as a means to achieve economic growth and overcome inequality. UNCTAD's 'Creative Economy' reports of 2008 and 2010 (though not 2013, which takes a somewhat different stance) reflect this discourse, arguing that despite the fact that many developing countries are still marginal players in terms of world cultural trade, with the right measures in place, the 'rich cultural heritage and inexhaustible pool of talent' that such countries possess will allow them to 'increase their shares of world trade and leap frog into new areas of wealth creation' (UNCTAD 2008: 1).

Whether this is in fact the case remains to be seen. That there is an inexhaustible variety of cultural activity in the world is unarguable, that much of it could have appeal beyond a local audience is clear, but the degree to which this leads to an equality of cultural trade and exchange is highly debatable. While almost anywhere can develop cultural products for global markets, those producers are held in a web of power relationships, with financial capital, investment and decision-making still concentrated in a few global centres. And then there is the question of scale: many cultural producers will never get to a size where the question of access to export markets or protection of intellectual property will be a real concern. For them, the more basic requirement is probably for skills, training and very small amounts of finance. This is not to suggest that the situation can never change – witness the rise of

Bollywood as a centre of the global film industry – but simply that the great variety of cultural expressions in the world should not be confused with equal access to a marketplace of consumers.

In his contribution to UNESCO's 2013 Creative Economy Report, Chris Gibson argues that the key to more balanced (if still far from equal) development of the global cultural economy is to recognise path dependency and the need for a pluralistic view of development. In other words, different industries in different contexts will have divergent paths and there is no single model – or even a few models – that they need to follow. The growth of popular cultural practices drawn from multiple global sources – Tanzanian hip hop, Mexican telenovellas, Nigerian moviemaking, South Korean pop music and so on – all attest to the growth of cultural production outside the traditional 'centres' of global cultural industries. Analysis of the Indian or Nigerian film industries, for example, shows very different trajectories to that of Hollywood, characterised by informal networks, localised funding and a more fragmented approach to ownership and distribution (Miller 2012; Mukherjee 2008).

Relatively few of these cases are explicitly policy-driven, though the Bollywood film industry was given its initial spur by policies of cultural protectionism, as India did not allow foreign films to be dubbed into Hindi until the 1990s (Hesmondhalgh 2013). An exception to this may be the case of South Korea, which has developed its popular cultural industries – film, television and music – in a concerted fashion sometimes known as the 'Korean wave'. Public funding for the development of fast broadband, for film and video-game production and to support an export drive, was accompanied again by protectionist policies at home; South Korea retains a screen quota policy which enforces a minimum number of screens/ screening times for domestically produced films at the cinema. Other countries such as France, Italy and Brazil have also used screen quotas and France in particular has supported the export of its popular culture wherever possible, but few have done it across the board – looking at domestic consumption, infrastructure and production – as successfully as Korea (Kwon and Kim 2013).

The notion of 'path dependency' suggests that history matters and that policy development, even at a global level, has to take account of the way in which particular cultural scenes were formed. Gibson gives the example of surfboard-making in Hawaii, which was 'exported' to other places, notably the USA and Australia by Hawaiian surfers, demonstrating their amazing skills. It seems unlikely that Hawaiian policymakers on a trade mission would have had the same success. Yet, while surfing is now popular in pretty much any country with a coastline, surfboard manufacture remains located in a few global centres, such as Hawaii, Australia, Indonesia and Brazil. In these places, deep subcultures of surfing have allowed a manufacturing industry to develop, based on social relationships, informal loans and sufficiently large tourist and surfing communities to act as consumers. The point is that policy initiatives and economic development are not enough without these local cultural factors; yet the creative economy model being pursued by UNCTAD and other agencies often appears insensitive to the time and the local knowledge required to understand and support such localised production centres.

CULTURE AND DEVELOPMENT

Alongside ideas of cultural trade and cultural diversity, the role of culture within development has long been of interest to agencies like UNCTAD and UNESCO. Clearly, 'development' includes economic development and thus many of the issues raised above, but what is sometimes referred to as 'social development' (Clammer 2012) or sustainable development refers to human development beyond the economic, including issues of education, health, political and civil rights and quality of life. These ideas informed the World Commission on Culture and Development, set up by the UN and UNESCO in 1993, and its 1995 report *Our Creative Diversity*, the opening statement of which was: 'Development divorced from its human or cultural context is growth without a soul' (WCCD 1995: 1). In this view, articulated by writers such as Amartya Sen (1999), culture is not simply a resource in the economic sense, nor is it a salve for particular social problems; it is an end in itself, a human quality valuable on its own terms because it enables humans to lead a dignified life and, crucially, helps them imagine what that life might mean for them. In many ways this view seems idealistic and not that far removed from what is sometimes seen as a European Romantic view of the importance of 'the arts' (see Chapter 2). But instead it draws absolutely on the anthropological view of culture as a whole way of life, not simply as a set of symbolic or artistic practices.

A recent UNESCO document, the Hangzhou Declaration, makes the case for culture as a fundamental pillar of human development, 'part of the global and local commons as well as a wellspring for creativity and renewal' (UNESCO 2013: 2). And in a speech to the UN General Assembly, Secretary General Ban Ki-Moon opined that 'too many well-intended development pro-grammes have failed because they did not take cultural settings into account' (quoted in UNESCO 2013: 9). Perhaps the most striking element of the 2013 Creative Economy Report is its stress on different pathways to development in strong contrast to what some have argued is the strongly neoliberalising tendency of cultural policy in recent years (including previous UN Creative Economy reports) to see the market as the 'natural' way of organising all economic activity and thus to prescribe similar policy approaches often in very different circumstances (Hesmondhalgh *et al.* 2014; McGuigan 2004). Instead, in words strongly influenced by Sen (1999), the report argues for development as 'a process that enhances the effective freedom of the people to pursue whatever they have reason to value' (UNESCO 2013: 16).

The 2013 Creative Economy Report thus seeks to articulate a slightly different approach to culture within development, one which complicates both our understanding of the 'economy' and our notion of the appropriate spatial level for such development to take place. The report notes that many of the policies developed in recent years, whether branded as 'creative industries' or 'creative economy', have taken as their model the de-industrialising cities of the Global North (see discussion of the creative city in Chapter 4) and this has often been inappropriate for cities or regions where the issues are very different and where coping with growth is more likely to be the paramount concern. The report thus suggests that 'comparisons along the South-South axis are likely to be more conducive to productive mutual learning in the Global South than the importation of ready-made models from elsewhere'

(UNESCO 2013: 35). This is important across a range of notions that typically accompany an understanding of culturally led economic development. Ideas of 'entrepreneurship' for example have a particular currency in places like East Africa where formal cultural institutions have less prominence and most cultural activity is entrepreneurially driven. However, the notion of 'entrepreneurship' as is sometimes understood in the Global North, framed in terms of individualism and ownership of intellectual property, may well not make sense in an East African context, where not only are intellectual property rights less likely to be strictly observed, but the very notion of 'ownership' may be differently understood.

Some writers have suggested that what the 'cultural economy' approach, which shaped the UNESCO report (despite its title), points to is that, rather than culture seeking to measure itself in economic terms, it might take an active role in redefining what we mean by the 'economic' itself. Chris Gibson has applied a cultural economy lens to his home country of Australia, which he describes as a 'settler nation, multicultural, with high per capita carbon emissions, as well as unresolved questions of Aboriginal sovereignty and self-determination' (Gibson 2012: 3). For him the study of the cultural economy allows us to disturb the categories of 'culture' and 'economy' and in particular to question the nature of 'the economy', a term which is often used in contemporary discourse as if it were a natural phenomenon rather than a social construction. The point is that what we understand as 'the economy' differs across cultures, as in the debate about Uluru mentioned above, where what is a 'resource' for tourism in one case is an uncommodifiable spiritual place in another. Across the Global South, many cultural pursuits that have hitherto been described as 'intangible cultural heritage', whether ceremonies, rituals or spiritual practices, are seen as continuous with other 'cultural activities' and thus form part of the 'cultural economy', an economy which includes a wide range of non-commercial cultural practices. Rather than seeing culture as a resource to be used economically, as the creative economy or cultural industries traditions generally do, the argument would be to see 'economic' resources from water to housing to green spaces in cultural terms, to help understand what they mean to people and hence how they can be valued in terms other than the economic – or through a radical rewriting of the definition of the economic.

The relevance of this for a study of international cultural policy is at least twofold. Not only does it disturb the notion of the 'nation' as the prime agent in favour of sub- or supranational groupings, which is particularly important when dealing with the question of Aboriginal or First Peoples or of the many groups whose 'cultures' do not fit neatly within national borders. It also links questions of cultural policy to others which are facing us as a global community, notably climate change, where national-level responses may be inadequate in a situation where particular cities and regions are more likely to be at risk. As we discussed in Chapter 5, questions of identity do not always fit neatly within national borders, and UNESCO's Creative Economy Report 2013 certainly suggests that different geographies matter when trying to understand the dense linkages that create culture. However, we should not assume that sub- or supranational groupings resolve question of identity any more easily, as the following section discusses.

REGIONAL GROUPINGS: THE CASE OF THE EU

To understand the challenges and limitations of international cultural policy, it is worth briefly returning to the cultural policies of a longstanding regional institution – in this case the European Union (EU). Despite supporting cultural programmes of one sort or another since the formation in the 1950s of what is now the European Union,[3] the EU still struggles with many of these issues: trade, diversity, localism and the tension between economic and other goals that are the subject of this chapter. In particular, the EU seems to struggle with profound questions of identity in its cultural policies; is there a common European heritage on which it can call, and if there is, how does this interact with the many non-European heritages of its citizens? Is there a European cultural identity or just a series of national identities and what should shape policy? To what extent should EU policy follow market dictates, or should it favour the cultural exception? While we have addressed the EU in Chapter 5, we return to it here in order to explore how the regional scale 'works' in international as well as national contexts (see Chapter 1 for discussion of the 'locating' of the region in scale terms).

The European Union secured limited legal 'competence' to act in culture in 1992, and its two stated objectives in this area are fostering diversity and fostering common cultural heritage; the tension that this might provoke being clear from the outset. Gordon (2010) argues that these possibly divergent aims make European cultural policy rather difficult to translate into clear and pragmatic policy objectives. The EU tends to favour high-flown rhetoric, particularly in its treaties, and in cultural terms often stresses what Lähdesmäki (2012: 62) calls the 'Great Past' of the continent, with reference to humanistic inheritances, freedom and democracy. The move from this rather selective account of Europe's past to actual policymaking is often clumsy and complicated, not least because the EU's institutional structures – the Council, Commission and Parliament – are sometimes at cross-purposes and indeed at odds with the interests of member states.

Nonetheless, the EU has become a significant policy player in culture, even if much of what it does in the cultural field is of a promotional rather than regulatory policy form (see Chapter 1). This includes artists' mobility programmes, prizes, awareness-raising events and perhaps best known of all, the European Capital of Culture event. European Capital of Culture (ECoC) has caught the imagination of policymakers and even some of Europe's citizens – at least in the cities chosen – to an extent rarely achieved by other EU cultural policy initiatives. Started in 1985, Capital (formerly City) of Culture was originally run as a competition, with a single city having the honour of being European City of Culture in a given year. The first wave of cities – Athens, Berlin, Paris – could be seen as representing traditional 'European' high culture, and indeed their years as cities of culture tended to concentrate on artistic events and festivals.

Glasgow, which was City of Culture in 1990, set a new model, that of the declining industrial city reinventing itself through culture, thus establishing the template for culture-led regeneration that dominated the next twenty years in Europe. Since 1999 there have been two cities each year and the 'competition' is intra-nation, the 2014 competition having been won by Riga in Latvia and Umea in Sweden. The 'contest' element means that the ECoC process resembles somewhat that for other mega events such as the Olympics or World Cup (though it carries nothing like the funding of either of these). Cities have been able to use ECoC to develop some of the urban cultural policy strands discussed in Chapter 4. As O'Brien argues (2013), response to a global policy context, a local belief in the power of culturally led regeneration, the opportunity for large-scale capital developments and an enthusiasm for 'evidence-based policy making' all came together in Liverpool's year as ECoC in 2008. The shift from a focus on ECoC as a celebration of the arts and heritage to its current status as an element of urban development policy has not been without its critics. Like other forms of culturally led regeneration, polarised forms of development have often occurred, with city centre areas benefitting from capital investment which eludes poorer neighbourhoods.

Many of its 'other' policies, such as Europe 2020,[4] the Bologna Process,[5] the European Social Fund[6] and Structural Funds, have cultural policy implications, consistent with the argument of this book that many of the public policies that have an impact on culture are not in fact 'cultural' policies at all. Via Structural Funds for example, the EU is often a significant funder of arts and culture, and indeed the 'creative cities' policy developments discussed in Chapter 4 were often part-funded by the EU, particularly in poorer regions of the continent.

More directly, it has been active in media and telecommunications policy, at least since the 1980s. The Television without Frontiers initiative (Commission of the European Communities 1984) was aimed at developing EU audio-visual industries, a response in part to the global dominance of the USA in this field. Hesmondhalgh (2013: 155) argues that these policies were 'ineffective and confused', setting quotas for non-EU TV imports but by using the qualifying phrase, 'if practicable', allowing such imports to flourish pretty much unhindered. Indeed, the EU strategy in media and communication has generally been to argue against the domination of a purely market-based approach to culture, while in practice supporting the development of its own large media corporations in this field, which it hopes will be able to compete on equal terms. Strategies that favour large media owners, however, tend to favour large media owners wherever they are located. Such firms are increasingly transnational (Hesmondhalgh 2013) and thus the EU's gestures towards public service or pubic interest media often lose out to policies that in practice help commercial media companies instead.

Thus, while the EU is large enough to be important in cultural policy terms, together with other regional groupings like Mercosur or Asean,[7] it struggles with the issue of identity and thus the legitimacy to act in matters of culture, where identity questions are often so pronounced. Undoubtedly, with its move in recent years towards a more pro-market, economically focussed cultural policy, in line with global political developments, it risks losing any distinctiveness it may once have had as the home of at least one of the major proponents of the cultural exception. Overall, as Miller comments, the citizens of Europe generally remain to be convinced that the EU's 'cultural policies are adding to their shared heritage, not just inventing it' (Lewis and Miller 2003: 269).

CULTURAL DIPLOMACY AND EXCHANGE

Next we want to consider the forms of cultural exchange that go beyond or sit adjacent to the strictly economic. Throsby (2010: 167) quotes the old adage, 'where culture leads, trade follows', and it is worth noting that although the term cultural 'exchange' is frequently used, it should not be taken to imply equity, as Braman's (2008) discussion of treaties in the art world makes clear. Nonetheless, it is apparent that promoting intercultural understanding and improving the image of a nation or community in the eyes of the world can have benefits beyond the economic. Culture is frequently a component of so-called 'soft power' (the ability to persuade through culture – values and ideas – as opposed to 'hard power', which conquers or coerces through military might (Nye 2004)). This reflects a longstanding diplomatic tradition, though given the growing importance of culture in the world economy, it casts it in a somewhat new guise. In addition, some argue that soft power is used by governments to improve their image not only abroad but also within the domestic sphere, to communicate to citizens, as Zhang's (2010) account of China's use of soft power suggests.

Cultural diplomacy, the exchange of ideas and artefacts between nations in order to foster greater understanding, seems to be becoming a favoured term to describe this ancient process (Nisbett 2012), though as Minnaert (2014) argues, the term contains an exquisite contradiction in that diplomacy is about the minimising of differences between places, while culture is often about the assertion of it. The degree to which it is a cultural policy *per se* – a chance to develop artistic reputations, ideas and new markets – or an element of foreign policy is disputed (Paschalidis 2009); the answer is probably both. As Melissa Nisbett (2012) has demonstrated in her account of the role of the British Museum in cultural diplomacy, even if the rationale is politically motivated, cultural institutions or workers may find it beneficial to take part in such exchanges for reasons of artistic expression or the chance to learn about other cultures and refresh one's own practice.

The degree to which artists feel comfortable taking part in cultural exchange and diplomacy, Nisbett (2012) writes, depends on how far they feel they can shape particular agendas and how powerful the cultural institutions are that they represent or work for. But it also depends on specific national histories, the problematic notion of 'official culture' as a programme of propaganda having greater resonance in some countries than others. As Wyszomirski *et al.* (2003) argue, while artists in the USA, the world's dominant cultural power, often display anxiety about the notion of taking part in what might be deemed official culture, countries like Brazil are willing to state that the Cultural Ministry is an important element of Brazilian diplomacy. This does not of course mean that US artists have not taken part in such processes; in one of the better-known examples of cultural diplomacy, the degree to which Abstract Expressionists such as Jackson Pollock and Barnett Newman were used as a tool of Cold War propaganda still animates debate and shapes perceptions (Stonor Saunders 1999).

In his article on how the Netherlands uses its cultural resources as soft power, Toine Minnaert (2014) reflects on what he sees as the tension between Dutch cultural policy, which has long prized freedom of expression as a core value, and foreign policy, which may be more conservative in defining what it sees as the Dutch image abroad. As Minnaert makes clear in his discussion of far-right politician Geert Wilders' film *Fitna*,[8] such controversial artistic expression, which celebrates its power to offend (in this case Muslims), is unlikely to be supported by a cultural policy focussed on diplomacy. But given the Netherlands' stated commitment to freedom of speech, not to mention the fact that *Fitna* was not funded by the Dutch government and they had no grounds for suppressing it, the government essentially had to wait out the controversy, supporting freedom of expression while asking Wilders to refrain from promoting his film (he did not refrain).

In analysing Dutch international cultural policy since the 1970s, Minneart sees shifts between an arts-oriented ICP, which seeks to project an image of Dutch national culture abroad, and one which seeks to use culture to safeguard Dutch economic interests – or 'empower international relations', in the words of a recent Dutch policy document (quoted in Minnaert 2014: 8). One issue which the policy has grappled with is the degree to which 'national identity' can ever be fixed enough or cohesive enough to be 'projected' at all, or in the case of the Netherlands whether ICP has to accommodate the often contradictory issues of national culture which the nation itself wrestles with.

Beyond embassies and national governments, one of the core mechanisms through which such exchanges are made possible are what Paschalidis (2009) calls 'cultural institutes', such as the Alliance Francais, Goethe Institute or Confucius Institute. In his account of such organisations, Paschalidis describes four distinct historical phases: cultural nationalism, propaganda, cultural diplomacy and what he calls cultural capitalism – the current phase. He argues that while often seen as 'colonial', an accusation which of course has some truth in the case of France and the UK, some institutions – particularly the Goethe Institute and the Dante Alighieri Society – were set up as part of nationalistic movements in their home countries of Germany and Italy in the late nineteenth century. Their target audience was often the diasporas of their people who they wished to enlist in the political project of unification.

The twentieth century saw governments start to take an active role in such institutes, hitherto voluntaristic in nature, with both Germany and Italy using their cultural institutes to spread fascist ideas in the 1930 and 1940s. In response to some extent, the British Council was established in 1934, while the USA established its first official programme of external cultural policy partly to counter the rise of fascism in Latin America. The post-war period saw a huge expansion of national cultural institutes, spurred on by the debates in UNESCO about the cultural exception and, in some cases, by the unprecedented rise of English as a global language: most institutes have language teaching as a core function – the Chinese government-backed Confucius Institute, established in 2004 in part to promote Mandarin learning, plans to have 1,000 centres open by 2020.

As Paschalidis (2009) argues, the end of the Cold War and the birth of a more multipolar world has given cultural institutes something of a boost. He cites the example of ex-Eastern bloc countries such as Hungary, Poland, the Czech Republic and Bulgaria, all of which have established new cultural industries since the fall of the Berlin Wall. The other recent development for such institutes is of course the development and export of the 'creative economy' discourse, with national branding and the export of national cultural products becoming of much greater concern than simply soft power and linguistic survival. The role of the British Council in the export of the DCMS's 'creative industries' idea is a case in point, as the Council has been active around issues such as cultural entrepreneurship and the various 'mapping studies' of the cultural industries across the world (see BOP Consulting 2010).

CONCLUSIONS

It is clear that the cultural products, services and practices are often distributed and consumed globally; but to what extent is it meaningful to talk about global or international cultural policy? This chapter has argued that while the agencies of international cultural policy – UNESCO, WIPO, UNCTAD and so on – may seem remote from the concerns of the average cultural producer or consumer, their activities increasingly shape the cultural environment. But perhaps more importantly, beyond those formal agencies a world of culture exchange beyond borders is now the norm.

That world of cultural exchange is not just nation to nation. Cities are significant agents of cultural policy and there exist several forums devoted to policy exchange between sites such as the Creative Cities Network or the World Cities Culture Forum.[9] Cultural institutions, particularly collecting institutions such as museums and galleries, have their own global networks and can help to shape international cultural policy as well as follow it (Nisbett 2012). And disapora networks are both a crucial market and a distribution system for films and music as well as non-commercial cultural goods.

International cultural policy is where we see both the commercial imperative at its most insistent, in debates about trade or intellectual property protection, but also the articulation of a whole set of cultural values that cut across or reshape ideas of trade, ownership and markets. It is in the international arena that many of the battles of twentieth-century cultural policy were fought, and in the twenty-first century we are seeing the emergence of new understandings of the role of culture within society, and new rationales for cultural investment that will produce a new framework for cultural policy.

***

We now want to briefly summarise and conclude the arguments made in the course of this book. The task we set ourselves was to outline some of the key issues in cultural policy and cultural policy research, to highlight key studies, and to critically engage with the scholarship in this field. We began by thinking through the definitional issues wrapped up in the apparently simple term 'cultural policy', thinking through in turn what the word 'culture' and then what the word 'policy' means. We explored how defining the 'culture' of cultural policy – the understanding of the reach and remit of cultural policy – has been hotly debated. We also showed how understandings of the 'culture' of cultural policy have changed over time with, for example, the coming of the 'creative industries' agenda. Our main aim in exploring what the 'policy' in cultural policy means was to reinforce the importance of locating cultural policy within the context of public policy more broadly (though even here we encountered some definitional conundrums). Studying cultural policy as policy can mean many things, and we have tried to sketch at least some of these out in this book.

Our attention then turned to our three spatial scales: to looking specifically at cultural policy in urban, national and international perspectives. While there are some significant overlaps between these scales, we hope to have shown that this kind of focus lets us see cultural policy working in different ways, too. And while it might seem as if the national scale has been doubly eclipsed, by the local on one hand and the global on another (Turner 2014), we have suggested that the nation-state is still an important focus for policy analysis. Overall, our aim in these three chapters has been to show that scale matters: that there is, as others have also pointed out, a geography to cultural policy. Or, rather, a series of geographies.

Our assessment of cultural policy in theory and in practice has inevitably been partial, guided by our own interests and blind-spots. We spent quite some time discussing issues of inclusion and exclusion, mindful of the fact that others will draw these boundaries in a different place. In some senses we have been quite 'traditional', focusing on cultural policy mainly through the arts and related sectors. We haven't said much about sport – despite the wedding of sport and culture in UK government. Likewise, we have said less than we might have done about the other sector wrapped up in the name of the DCMS: the media. We have drawn in examples from policy work in these areas, but perhaps to less of an extent than others would have done. There are choices that have to be made. While critics have sometimes worried about this fact and been troubled by the consequences of the choices made by particular scholars (e.g. Bennett 2004), we're less concerned with boundary patrols and more interested in making connections. We're also particularly keen to restate the quote from Toby Miller and George Yudice (2002: 34) that we used right at the start of this book: 'getting to know cultural policy and intervening in it is an important part of participating in culture'. It is entirely in the spirit of this statement that we have worked our way through the material and issues that make up *Cultural Policy*.

NOTES

1 Regional free trade area comprising Argentina, Brazil, Venezuela, Paraguay and Uruguay, founded in 1991.
2 Dumping refers to the practice whereby good are sold at lower that the cost of production or lower than they are sold in their home territory in order for a country to establish a market advantage in another country.
3 The EU began as the European Coal and Steel Community (ECSC) in 1951, changing its name to the European Economic Community (EEC) in 1958 and becoming the European Union in 1993. In the intervening years it has grown in size by the accession of new member states and in power by the addition of policy areas to its remit.
4 Europe 2020 is a wide-ranging plan for the economic development of the EU.
5 The name given to a series of meetings and agreements on the convergence of European Higher Education standards and qualifications.
6 A programme to improve employment and job opportunities in the EU
7 Association of South East Asian Nations.
8 *Fitna* is a short film of 2008, which tries to argue that the Qu'ran motivates its followers to hate those who do not accept Islamic teaching.
9 See www.worldcitiescultureforum.com/.

REFERENCES AND FURTHER READING

Allard, G. (2007) 'Imagined diversity', *International Journal of Cultural Policy*, 13(1): 71–84.

Bennett, O. (2004) 'The torn halves of cultural policy research', *International Journal of Cultural Policy*, 10(2): 237–48.

Braman, S. (2008) 'International treaties and art', *International Journal of Cultural Policy*, 14(3): 315–33.

BOP Consulting (2010) *Mapping the Creative industries: a Toolkit*, London: British Council.

Clammer, J. (2012) *Culture, Development and Social Theory: Towards an Integrated Social Development*. London: Zed Books.

Commission of the European Communities (1984) *Television without Frontiers*, Green Paper, Brussels: CEC. Embodied in Council Directive 89/552/eec.

Cowen, T. (1998) *In Praise of Commercial Culture*, Cambridge MA: Harvard University Press.

Cunningham, S. (2009) 'Trojan Horse or Rorschach Blot? Creative industries discourse around the world', *International Journal of Cultural Policy*, 15(4): 375–86.

Feigenbaum, H. (2010) 'The political economy of cultural diversity in film and tele-vision', in J. Singh (ed.) *International Cultural Policies and Power,* Basingstoke: Palgrave MacMillan.

Gibson, C. (2012) 'Cultural Economy: Achievements, Divergences, Future Pro-spects', *Geographical Research,* 50(3): 282–290.

Gordon, C. (2010) 'Great expectations – the European Union and cultural policy: fact or fiction?' *International Journal of Cultural Policy,* 16(2): 101–20.

Held, D. (2005) *Debating Globalization,* Cambridge: Polity.

Held, D. and McGrew, A. (eds) (2000) *The Global Transformations Reader.* Cambridge: Polity.

Herman, D. and McChesney, R. (1997) *The Global Media,* London: Cassell.

Hesmondhalgh, D. (2013) *The Cultural Industries,* third edition. London:Sage.

Hesmondhalgh, D., Nisbett, M., Oakley, K. and Lee, D. (2014) 'Were New Labour's cultural policies neo-liberal?' *International Journal of Cultural Policy,* online first.

Kwon, S.-H. and Kim, J. (2013) 'The cultural industry policies of the Korean government and the Korean Wave', *International Journal of Cultural Policy,* online first.

Lähdesmäki, T. (2012) 'Rhetoric of unity and cultural diversity in the making of European cultural identity', *International Journal of Cultural Policy,* 18(1): 59–75.

Lewis, J. and Miller, T. (eds) (2003) *Critical Cultural Policy Studies. A Reader,* Oxford: Blackwell.

McGuigan, J. (2004) *Rethinking Cultural Policy,* Maidenhead: Open University Press.

Miller, J. (2012) 'Global Nollywood: the Nigerian movie industry and alternative global networks in production and distribution', *Global Media and Communication,* 8(2): 117–33.

Miller, T., Govil, N., McMurria, J. and Maxwell, R. (2004) *Global Hollywood,* London: BFI.

Miller, T. and Yudice, G. (2002) *Cultural Policy,* London: Sage.

Minnaert, T. (2014) 'Footprint or fingerprint: international cultural policy as identity policy', *International Journal of Cultural Policy,* online first.

Mukherjee, A. (2008) 'The audio-visual sector in India', in D. Barrowclough and Z. Kozul-Wright (eds) *Creative Industries and Developing Countries: Voice, Choice and Economic Growth,* London: Routledge.

Nisbett, M. (2012) 'New perspectives on instrumentalism: an empirical study of cultural diplomacy', *International Journal of Cultural Policy,* online first.

Nye, J. (2004) *Soft Power: the Means to Success in World Politics,* Cambridge MA: Perseus.

O'Brien, D. (2013) *Cultural Policy: Management, Value and Modernity in the Creative Industries,* London: Routledge.

Paschalidis, G. (2009) 'Exporting national culture: histories of Cultural Institutes abroad', *International Journal of Cultural Policy,* 15(3): 275–89.

Pyykkönen, M. (2012) 'UNESCO and cultural diversity: democratisation, commodi-fication or governmentalisation of culture?' *International Journal of Cultural Policy,* 18(5): 545–62.

Sen, A. (1999) *Development as Freedom,* Oxford: Oxford University Press.

Shuker, R. (1994) *Understanding Popular Music*, London: Routledge.

——(2003) *Understanding Popular Music*, London: Routledge.

Stonor Saunders, F. (1999) *Who Pays the Piper? The CIA and the Cultural Cold War*, London: Granta.

Throsby, D. (2010) *The Economics of Cultural Policy*, Cambridge: Cambridge University Press.

Tunstall, J. (1994) *The Media are American*, second edition, London: Constable.

Turner, G. (2014) 'Culture, politics and the cultural industries: reviving a critical agenda', in K. Oakley and J. O'Connor (eds) *The Routledge Companion to the Cultural Industries*, London: Routledge.

UNCTAD (2008) *The Creative Economy Report: The Challenge of Assessing the Creative Economy: Towards Informed Policy-Making*, New York: UNCTAD. Available at http://unctad.org/en/docs/ditc20082cer_en.pdf (accessed 14/03/14).

——(2010) *The Creative Economy Report: Creative Economy: A Feasible Development Option*, New York: UNCTAD.

UNESCO (2013) *The Creative Economy Report: Widening Local Development Pathways*, New York: UNESCO.

WCCD (1995) *Our Creative Diversity: Report of the World Commission on Culture and Development*, Paris: UNESCO. Available at http://unesdoc.unesco.org/images/0010/001016/101651e.pdf (accessed 20/11/13).

Wyszomirski, M., Burgess, C. and Peila, C. (2003) *International Cultural Relations: a Multi-Country Comparison*, Columbus OH: Cultural Diplomacy Research Series, Ohio State University.

Zhang, W. (2010) 'China's cultural future: from soft power to comprehensive national power', *International Journal of Cultural Policy*, 16(4): 383–402

INDEX

Page numbers in **bold** indicate reference to a table.